Daniel J. Strawbridge

CHILCOMPTON
IN FOCUS
TWO

by

DAVID J. STRAWBRIDGE

CHILCOMPTON

1994

Another book and a further look
at the life of yesteryear
When people worked hard by hook and not crook
For the things that they held dear

The hardship and suffering our forebears went through
For the generations ahead to enjoy
Could all be for nothing, at least that's my view
If God is forgotten and greed we employ

So browse through this book please, make up your own mind
About folk that you see who died hoping to find
A new life beyond where there's nothing amiss
Except tears of nostalgia as they reminisce

But don't lets despair, there is much we can do
With a new school, plus churches and halls (yes two)
People seem happy and children's faces beam
Particularly at the ducks on our lovely stream.

©1994 D. J. Strawbridge
Davanda, Chilcompton, Bath BA3 4EW

British Library Cataloguing in Publication Data:
A catalogue record for this book is available from the British Library

Chilcompton In Focus two
1. Somerset. Chilcompton, history
1. Strawbridge, David J.
942.3'83

ISBN 0 9510788 3 6

Origination and Production by Avonset, Midsomer Norton, Bath.
Printed at St Andrews Press of Wells.

Contents

Cover photographs:
St. Vigor & St. John C.E.V.A. Primary School, half built behind the Village Hall, Wells Road (Opened January 1993)
Chilcompton V.C. Infants School, Church Lane (Closed December 1992).
Downside V.A. Junior School, Stockhill Road, (Closed December 1992).

Foreword

WHEN I was asked to write this foreword to "Chilcompton in Focus Two" it occurred to me what a debt the village of Chilcompton owes to David. To produce one book "Meandering through Chilcompton" then "Chilcompton in Focus One" and now "Chilcompton in Focus Two" will leave the village with a record of families and occasions that will be of great importance to future generations. The difficulty he has had even after a relatively short time to get names to fit all the faces shows that links with the past quickly fade. If the task David has undertaken had been left another generation there is no doubt that many fewer names would have been at the foot of the pictures. Today photography is very much a way of life and I think an important lesson we could all learn is the importance of putting the names and dates on the back of the photographs themselves so that future historians will have an easier job to record past events. I have great pleasure in commending this book to all.

Desmond Mattick

Preface

THIS is my third major book and my enthusiasm has thankfully not yet begun to wane. It is five years since I published Focus One and during that time Chilcompton has lost an alarming number of elderly folk and these were the people most able to help me by supplying pictures and identifying persons. Therefore my chosen hobby becomes more difficult as time goes by.

I must say that everyone has been most helpful and polite even when I have called at inconvenient times. Some have gone to a lot of trouble to solve problems for me.

You may remember how misfortune seems to befall people delving into Chilcompton's past but thankfully this appears to have eased and there is only a heart attack shrugged off by my brother, Ron, to report apart from a longstanding tendon problem with my daughter-in-law's hand.

Two new estates in the village have been completed: one is council owned at Parsonage Lane called Golledge Close, and the other is Carter's Way just off the main Wells Road. Both are nicely named after two men (not forgetting their wives) who did so much for Chilcompton. The next important building project is likely to be on the site of Sheppards Saw Mill which will be a big improvement. There appears to be a profound lack of bungalows when one considers the demand.

I hope you will find something of interest in Focus Two. I already have a good number of pictures which I could put towards a Focus Three so if readers have pictures of interest I would still like to borrow them. I am still finding lovely pictures of families, groups and individuals which are now obsolete because owners forgot to write names and dates on the back, so please get to work and sort out those drawers and shoeboxes where so much history is hidden.

Meandering through Chilcompton (MTC) and Chilcompton in Focus One are still available. I hope you enjoy reading Focus Two.

ADDENDUM. Some pictures have an (a) and (b). These are photos which I included too late to change the numbering.

This book is dedicated to three of my four children who have not received a mention namely – Cheryl, Bryony and Dominic.

Acknowledgements

TO EVERYONE in the village and from outside, my sincere thanks and appreciation for all your old pictures and snaps. I hope those whose names are not listed below will accept my thanks for their help and my apologies for omission.

As usual my wife Audrey has had to put up with my absence for hours on end but has always helped and encouraged me even after forty years of marriage so my very special thanks to her. Also to my sister-in-law Joan who also read everything and suggested useful additions.

Many thanks also to Philip Waite for the excellent cover photographs plus two other aerial pictures of the Court Hotel and Downside R.C. School. Thanks again to Chris Howell, Ivo Peters, Fr Philip Jebb, Dr Warwick Rodwell, Robin Atthill, Tom Bush, Sir Michael Armitage, Wendy Walker and the Media in Wessex Press. Also to Desmond Mattick, Chairman of the Parish Council for his kind foreword. Roy Pointing and Dennis Horler were a good source of help and encouragement. The Parish Council, The Chilcompton Society and The Golden Hour were also very helpful.

Thanks are warmly extended to the following for their photographs or assistance.

Muriel Aulich, Mary Ashman, Judy Andrews, Pat Brady, Ruth & Harry Bevan, Gwen Bailey, Ethel Brommell, Alb Bailey, Minnie Bryant, Ted Bennett, Jean Brooks, Barbara Bush, Hilda & Trevor Bailey, Ivan Burge, David & Cynthia Brown, Madge Baker, Win Burge, Pam Blacker, Basil Banwell, Colin & Marlene Carver, Glyn & Sheila Carver, Wilf & Brian Carver, Lana & Duncan Carver, Molly Bennett, Norman & Rosalie Carpenter, Lily Clark, Chris & Muriel Colbourne, Mike Collis, Mary Charles, Doug Chivers, John & Beulah Challenger, Henry Charles, John Church, Maureen Coombs, Gwen Camden, John & Pat Cherrett, Margaret Candy, Ciss Cornick, Geoff Coles, Mike Carter, Jim Coles, Gordon & Margaret Curtis, Joan Clarke, Linda Corp, Cilla Cooper, Dennis Chedgy, Jack & Margaret Clare, Keith Coombes, Maureen neé Davidge, Ivor Davis, Pam Dix, Ray & Norma Dando, Ruth Dunford, Hilary Edwards, Phyllis Edwards, Johanna Edwards, John & Wendy Earle, John & Norman Emery, Edna Ford, Frank & Rosemary Foxwell, Mervyn & Barbara Fowler, Maurice Fisher, Ivan, Violet, Don & Linda Gumbleton, Nora Gilson, Ada Gilson, George & Jo Golledge, Edgar Gane, Frances Greenway, Susan & Mavis Gibbings, Ada Gardner, Rose Gibbings, John Gray, Hilda Guy, Ivy Gullick, Betty Gould, Eve Holland, Vera Harris, Joan Howell, Gerald Heal, Ivy Horler, Ellen Hiscocks, Mary & Philip Heal, Pat Hembry, Susan Harris, Den & Joan Hartley, Barry & Christine Hartley, Bill Humphries, Hugh Hodges, Derek Hunt, Ivor Hann, Elsie Jones, Elsie Jennings, Lily James, Bill & Pearl Kelly, Rachael Kuzemka, Len Kerton, Cyril & Ann Leach, Nancy Lawrence, Nelson & Betty Lane, Sid & Jane Lawrence, Terry & Sally Moore, John & Janet Moore, Jim & Gwen Moore, Olive Mitchell, Tony & Diana Merrick, Ray & Irene Matthews, Desmond & Betty Mattick, Wally & Richard Moon, Dave & Gwen Mackay, Ralph Macdonald, Paul & Julia McKeivor, Bert Monckton, Jane Mooney, Albert & Hilda Noel, Carrie Obern, Dennis Obern, Gordon & Pam Patch, Alice & Heather Perkins, Cliff, Wilf and Betty Perkins, Joe Pugh, Joan Pugsley, Arthur Perkins, Joan Painting, Grahame & Marlene Pickford, Mabel Plumley, Bill & Frank Pointing, Leslie Ponting, Barbara Pain, David & Sylvia Rogers, Percy Rogers, Michael & Joan Saul, Jean Schuster, Alban & Nancy Seymour, Dorothy Schmid, Frank Stock, Ron Strawbridge, Lauren Strawbridge, Gary Scammell, Jack & Vern Stuckey, Olive Sobey, Ted Seviour, Gilb Selway, Eric, Bill & Eileen Sheppard, Stan Shearn, Leslie Smailes, Ruth Smith, Terry & Sally Sage, Olive, Nora, Mary, Harry, Jack, Laurie, Fred, Win, Jim, Alice, Joe & Reg Targett, Revd. S. Tudgey, Victoria Taylor, Audrey (Ciss) Thomas, Joan Turner, Iris & Colin Trainor, Heather Uphill, Ron Uphill, Margery Vinnell, Reg Virgin, Ivan, Mary & Rodney Veale, Nigel, Grace, Josie & Mildred Wood, Jack, Phyllis & Trevor Witcombe, John & May Webb, Bert & Joyce Webber, Grace Witcombe, Connie Wellington, Jane Winsley, Mary Williams, Diane & Graham Young. Finally, a thankyou to my printer Roger Williamson of Avonset who has been extremely helpful.

Chilcompton Church and School

1 As usual I like to put the church first and this is a pleasing picture of St. John's with an abundance of trees large and small. It was taken probably around 1910 when the Church was the hub of village life and the time when families were large, wages small, but Sunday was always special. This scene is now less picturesque with the 1991 church hall abutting onto the churchyard but it is a well-built hall and very useful.

2 Inside the church looking west the occasion is Harvest Festival probably between 1900 and 1910. The font in the bellringing chamber and the pillars in the nave are decorated for the celebration. The bellringing chamber was formerly one floor up and the ringers would climb an inside stairway fixed to the south wall which was also the access to the pre-1839 musicians' and singers' gallery at the rear of the nave. A metal tie holding the floor can be seen on picture 6.

NEW SCHOOL, CHILCOMPTON.

3 The title is 'New School' and this picture was probably taken about 1876 after the school had been re-built. A point of interest is that the footpath one used to enter the "Withy Beds" is clearly shown on the right of the foreground.

THE SCHOOL, CHILCOMPTON.

4 This school photo shows a lot of foliage, an entrance gate to the farmyard and a stile for public use. The school bell, (upper right) is now at the new 1993 school behind the village hall.

5 Taken in 1889 at the rear of the school before an extra classroom was added (1894) are perhaps half the pupils of the school pictured with their Head Teacher, Miss Bertha Long (left). It is too long ago to name anyone else with certainty, but some of the descendants of these pupils are certain to live locally and may be able to see a likeness here and there.

6 Another group c.1893 with Miss Alice Sheppard, teacher, on extreme left with her hands on her young brother's shoulders—James E. Sheppard. The teacher back left is probably Winifred Pearce with Bertha Long on the right. The location is by the church tower.

7 Dancing around the Maypole in 1920 the pupils forget the strict school discipline for the time being. The cottage behind was demolished in the 1950's.

8 Mr Knight, 1910–14, became headteacher (from 50 applicants) on the retirement of Miss Bertha Long. He is pictured here with his top class in 1913 when there were over 130 pupils. For years I tried to find names for this picture but all I could acquire are—left to right rear—2nd boy Leonard Dunford, (4) Bill Holder, (5) Bill Horler, (7) Reg Burnett. Middle row—(4) Eva Singer. Front row—(1) Tom Targett, (2) Reg and (3) Ron Beck(Twin), (6) Evelyn and (7) Olive Eyles (Twin), (8) Harry Veale.

9 Outside the school c.1952. By the lamp post a milk churn is ready for collection from Brook House Farm (Eddie Bevan). Front six kneeling or bending——(1) Alan Fletcher, (2) Tom Jones, (3) Bob Brown, (4) John Brown, (5) Donald Gumbleton, (6) Adrian Carver (bending). Back row——(1) Bill Quinn, (2) Stan Mogg (3) Dave Brown, (4) John Gumbleton, (5) Trevor Davis (6) Michael Pike, (7) David Mattick, (8) Victor Brown, (9) Peter Padfield, (10) Les Dunford, (11) Lilburn Burge, (12) Bill Vaughan, (13) Colin Trainor.

10 All smiles from the pupils in c.1955. On the right is headteacher Mrs Edna Gunning (1955–68).On the left is Mrs Marie Cook (nee Hodges) who left the school in 1957 and started, in 1969, her own nursery school at home in Chestnut Barn, Parsonage Lane. Marie died in 1975.

Back row—(1) Mrs Marie Cook, (2) Donald Gumbleton, (3) David Box, (4) Barrie Lovell, (5) Ian Horler, (6) Paddy Lane, (7) David Gumbleton, (8) Martin Perkins, (9) ? Brown, (10) Adrian Carver, (11) David Adnett, (12) Terry Jeffery, (13) Brian Pike, (14) John Brown, (15) Basil Carver, (16) Fred Purnell, (17) Trevor Brown, (18) Mrs Edna Gunning.

Third row—(1) Margaret Purnell, (2) Maureen Purnell, (3) Stephenie Fletcher, (4) Pauline Moon, (5) Pam Box, (6) Mary Davis, (7) ?, (8) Christine Lovell, (9) Hilary Winfield, (10) Rita Golledge, (11) Carol Eyles, (12) Andrea Horler, (13) ?, (14) Susan Jones, (15) Linda Purnell, (16) Jennifer Dally.

Second row—(1) Margaret Dunford, (2) Sheila Box (3) ?, (4) ?, (5) Christine (Sally) Lane, (6) ?, (7) Marlene Holder, (8) Joy Golledge, (9) Lucy Promel, (10) Cynthia Charles, (11) Dawn Eyles, (12) Mary Brown, (13) Irene Jones.

Front row—(1)?, (2) Michael Trainer, (3) Ray Purnell, (4) David Purnell, (5) Eric Horler, (6) ?, (7) Chris Durrant, (8) Chris Dally, (9) Jack Dunford, (10) David Promel, (11) Ramond Uhl, (12) Michael Swift, (13) Richard Moon, (14) Glyn Carver.

The school was closed in Dec. 1992 and sold on 1st June 1993 by the trustee, the Archdeacon of Wells, to Paul and Julia McKeivor for £60,000. A great deal of work was necessary to convert the building to a private house but this has now been achieved in a sensitive and tasteful manner. Inside there are now three bedrooms upstairs, a dining room, sitting room, games room, two bathrooms, and plenty of space. Externally the building remains unaltered and still impressive with its white lias stone walls, strong buttresses and large domed windows. Paul and Julia with their two children moved in on 1st Nov. 1993.

Stockhill Church and School

11a The nave, gallery and organ at Christ Church, Stockhill Road.

11b Part of the nave and chancel. Photo's a and b were taken after the last service held at 10.30am on the 12th June 1983 and both can be compared with No. 100 in Focus One to see changes including the re-siting of the organ.

11c A close-up taken in August 1966 of the chancel of Christ Church.

12   The Reverend Lionel Greenway, vicar from 1944 to 1980. Died 1983.

13 Some of the choir in the 1950's. (1) Trevor Bailey, (2) Jim Stacey (Churchwarden), (3) Ted Greenway (Lionel's Father), (4) Rev'd Lionel, (5) Mary Greenway, (6) Barbara Bailey, (7) Bill Gibbings, (8) Barry Clarke, (9) Bert Gibbings, (10) Carrie Obern(Organist).

14 Some of the Sunday School Class c.1950. Standing—(1) Barbara Bailey, (2) Maureen Davidge, (3) Mary Greenway (Teacher), (4) Derek Eels, (5) Ivan Gumbleton. Seated—(1) Barry Clarke, (2) Terry Whitehead, (3) ?.

15 School children performing country dancing on the Vicarage Lawn during the Garden Fete of 1960.

16 A south view of Stockhill School during the 1940's. The blockwall protecting the rear door had been built in 1940 as a safeguard against bomb blast.

17 A west view of the school after modernisation in 1967.

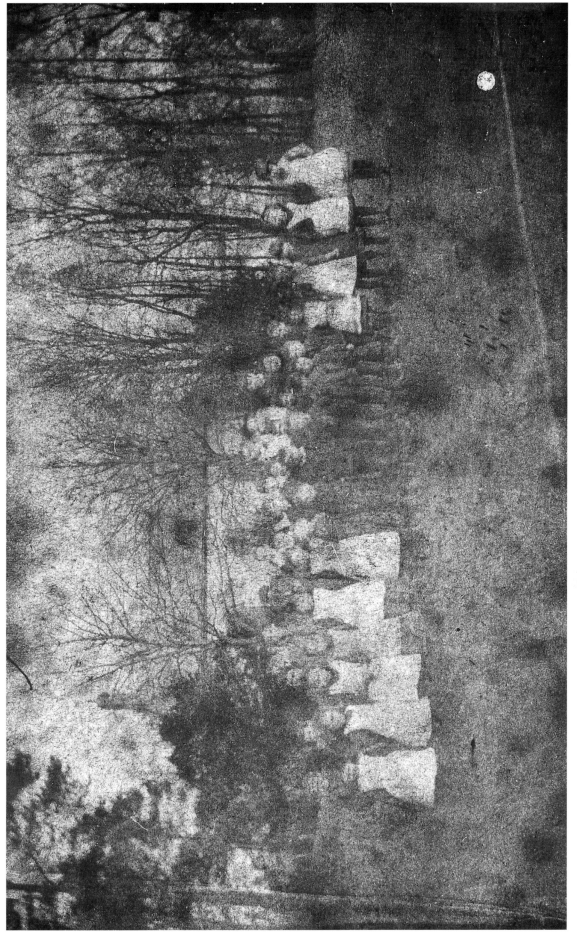

18 A very faded picture this but still interesting. It was taken on 5.2.1886 in the paddock between the church and the school before it became a cemetary. Some teachers and the Rev'd William Leay are in the group of school children and the church is in the background.

19 Four teachers are present in this early picture at the school in 1887. The building was enlarged in 1895 and again in 1912. The pupils lived mostly either in the Downside Parish part of Chilcompton or in the Moorewood area. Three teachers at the time were Mrs J. Jones, Lucy Emery and Annie Cox.

20 Headteacher Mr James Brunker Taylor 1899–1911 with his wife (left) and daughters Blanche, (centre), and Queenie, (right), c.1910. Mr Taylor died after his bicycle collided with a motorbike at the Street/Parsonage Lane junction (see No. 40) in July 1911. He was 70.

21 An earlier (c.1900) picture of Mr Brunker Taylor with teachers Blanche Robbins, Ellen Bissex and pupils taken on the same day as 102 in Focus One.

22 Headteacher Mr William Bowers (right) with his 1915 top class eighth in the middle row is Queenie Richards who had started at the school as a child, became a monitress 1916, assistant teacher 1921, married Len Emery 1926, and become headteacher 1952. A few other names are—Back row—(1) ?, (2) George Foxwell, (3) ?, (4) ?, (5) ?, (6) Jim Stacey, (7) Fear, (8) ?, (9) ?. Middle row—(1) Llewellyn, (2) Pearl Arthurs, (3) Reg Coles, (4) Etta Lewis, (5) ?, (6) ?, (7) ?, (8) Queenie Richards, (9) Susan Coles, (10) Foxwell, (11) ?, (12) Kathleen Gait, (13) Emily Milbourne. Front row—(1) ?, (2) Hill, (3) Peppard, (4) Maggie Llewellyn, (5) Bill Gibbings, (6) Len Shearn, (7) Fear, (8) ?, (9) Padfield, (10) ?, (11) ?.

23 Group 3 in 1921. Names—Back row—(1) Ken Pearson, (2) Arthur Gilson, (3) Mervyn Padfield, (4) Bill Ridout, (5) Harry Fear, (6) ?, (7) Alec Perry, (8) Jim Fear. Middle row—(1) Harry Stephens, (2) Gwen Witcombe, (3) Phyllis Gould, (4) Mary Derrick, (5) Joan Gait, (6) Evelyn Veasey, (7) Leslie Ridout. Front row—(1) ? Salter, (2) Gwen Frampton, (3) Sarah (Sally) Llewellyn, (4) Ethel Emery, (5) Mildred (Queenie) Gray, (6) Liza (Betty) Foxwell, (7) Phillip Stephens.

24 A mainly tight-lipped class in 1957. Names are—Mrs Queenie Emery.—Back row—(1) Alan Crawford, (2) Clive Jones, (3) Peter Gould, (4) Colin Maidment, (5) Nigel Hicks, (6) Raymond Powell, (7) Michael Whittock, (8) John Miles, (2) Gillian Baker, (3) Judith Hicks, (4) Denise Maggs, (5) Jackie Jones, (6) Sarah Selway, (9) D. Bay. Middle row—(1) John Miles, (2) Gillian Baker, (3) Judith Hicks, (4) Denise Maggs, (5) Jackie Jones, (6) Susan Bailey, (7) Wendy Miles, (8) Delia Robbins, (9) Marilyn Scammell, (10) Andrew Moss. Front row—(1) Suzanne Scammell, (2) Dawn Purnell, (3) Sarah Selway, (4) Susan Ball, (5) Bernadette Dando, (6) Jean Heal, (7) Margaret Heal, (8) Judith Painting.

25 This 1959 Junior Class didn't know it but it was probably the best time in their lives. Names—Back row—(1) Peter Gould, (2) Ian Eyles, (3) Philip Webber, (4) Colin Maidment, (5) John Young, (6) William Stock, (7) James de Costabadie, (8) Hilary Sheppard, (9) John Karnaus. Middle row Standing—(1) Lynn Wilcox, (2) Olwyn Moore, (3) Delia Robbins, (4) Dawn Purnell, (5) Marilyn Scammell, (6) Pat Warren, (7) Sarah Earle. Middle row Sitting—(1) Jane Perkins, (2) Cynthia Charles, (3) Jean Heal, (4) Judith Painting, (5) Margaret Heal, (6) Jane Sheppard, (7) Bernadette Dando, (8) Janet Manning. Front row—(1) Clive Jones, (2) John Miles, (3) Andrew Moss, (4) Lance Charlton, (5) David Whittock, (6) Alan Jones.

26 Infants class in 1961. Names—Back row—(1) Kevin Charles, (2) Garnett Banwell, (3) ?, (4) Roger Wilcox, (5) Sandra Stuckey, (6) Julian Reakes, (7) Yvonne Banwell, (8) Gary Scammell. Middle row Standing—(1) Barbara Gulliford, (2) Peter Strawbridge, (3) Gillian Clark, (4) James Karnous, (5) Hilary de Costabadie, (6) Karl Schuster, (7) Lynn Hiscox, (8) Hilary Charlton. Middle row Sitting—(1) Avril Hiscox, (2) Rachel Sheppard, (3) Ruth Gulliford, (4) Geoffrey Sheppard, (5) Laurence Eyles, (6) ?, (7) John Bailey. Front row—(1) Ann Bailey, (2) David Wilcox, (3) Margaret Beacham, (4) Andrew Bailey, (5) June Maidment, (6) Michael Heal.

27 Group of happy leavers in 1961. Back Three—(1) Philip Webber, (2) James de Costabadie, (3) John Karnous. Front row—(1) Roderick Person, (2) Alan Jones, (3) Janet Mannings, (4) Lance Charlton.

28 Mrs Queenie Emery at her retirement party in December 1961 having been at the school for 55 years. Left to right—Stephen Schuster, Sandra King, Margaret Heal, Albert Bryant, Richard Eyles (boy) Olwyn Moore, Jean Heal. Faces behind bouquet—Michael Heal, Mary Heal. Extreme right—Sandra Stuckey.

29 The day of the school Christmas Lunch 1985. Back row (kitchen staff)—Christine Hartley, Olive Sobey, Jane Coles and Mildred Wood. Front row (teaching staff)—Katherine Silvester, Richard Bullard, Joy Buckerfield, Joanne Byrne, Margaret Dera.

30 Cycling proficiency class. Sitting—Amanda Toms. With bicycles—Katie Cotton and Lee Rogers. Others left to right—Sarah Wilcox, Sarah Brown, James Silvester, Trudy Pike, Zena Bishop, Joy Buckerfield (Instructor), Matthew Scott, Paul Lyons, Andrew Eyles, Jason Pike, Richard Waite, David Hodgkinson.

31 Come on the reds! The school football team. Back row—Robert Hayne, Brendon Andrews, Peter Moore, Steven Lyons, David Hodgkinson, Ian Crick. Front row—Paul Box, James Silvester, Nick Davis, James Hayne, James Sheppard.

Village Scenes

32 At the foot of Coach Lane stood two very old coach houses, or cart sheds as they were more commonly known. This one stood on the north side of the road and shows the east-facing entrance. On the left of the picture is the stile post for the Clapton footpath.

33 This smaller coachhouse, again facing east, stood on the other side of the lane which can be seen passing on the right. These pictures complement No. 28 in Focus One.

34 The scene in this early picture of Shell House frontage (it can be compared with a slightly earlier one on page 74 MTC) has changed little except for the horse and breadvan at the foot of Norton Down Lane. It is nice to see the Post Box still in the same position in 1994.

35a Two more pictures of commemoration day at the Church House 18th July 1914. (This is covered in more detail in Focus One pages 8 to 11.) The cottages in the background are in The Pitching.

35b Lady Kathleen Thynne straightens up for a photo after laying her commemoration plaque. The Church House was dedicated and declared open on 14.10.1916.

36 A front view of Shell House in 1964 taken from the steps of Church House after morning Sunday School. Notice the fine stone shell or scallop over the front door and the nicely trained cotoneaster on the right. The two children are my daughters Lauren 4 years old and Cheryl 5 (facing).

37 Attached to the rear of Shell House was a farm cottage (with porch) which had formerly been servants quarters and kitchens. Linked to the cottage (left) is the former parish hall, now demolished.

38 A further 1954 view of the old parish hall which always belonged to the owners of Shell House but was available for village use. Featured with the cow are Paulene (Pip) Lawrence and an Aunt Gert and Uncle Ken from Dorset with young Ken Eyles from Brickyard, Midsomer Norton. Sid and Pip farmed a dairy herd and 36 acres from 1952–58. (MTC90)

39a and 39b Pictures of the ruinous state of the old coachhouse, stables and dairy belonging to Shell House. This building has been tastefully converted into a private house whereas Shell House is now three separate units. A description of this building can be found on 126 in Focus One.

The Street Stilcompton. No 2.

40 One of many pictures taken of this scene and showing the former busy grocery/off licence shop. One cottage has since been demolished to effect an access.

41 Eagle House, formerly the servants quarters to nearby Gainsborough House. This has for a long time been one of the best houses in Chilcompton. A stone eagle is above the porch. Reclining are two sisters, Theodosia Emery (left), and Victoria Maud Oakes—now Mrs Taylor and in her 98th year.

42 Young Jim Reeves surveys a pleasing view of the ducks on the stream—which makes an S bend at this point—the forecourt of Eagle House.

THE STREET, CHILCOMPTON.

43 Taken from the drive-in entrance to Eagle House is this early view of the Street ponds and a wooded area of the field always known as 'front ground' which extended to the Britannia Inn in the background.

44 The most photographed part of the village much altered over the centuries with the coming and going of Norton Hall just past the tall tree on the left. The Britannia Inn is on the right. The inquisitive cow stands on the site of a former Malthouse. Mervyn Emery (born 1911) leans on the railings. Two nice hayricks can just be seen in the paddock (centre left).

The Street, Chilcompton. No.1.

45 Looking back down the Street, Gainsborough House can just be seen. It is suggested the occupants of the trap are Fred and Martha Reeves, who lived in the Post Office which can be seen in the centre background on 44.

46 A similar position but more detail. Twenty young folk pose by the Street Ponds with Norton Hall Cottage prominent and Eagle House beyond. On the left is the L–shaped Gainsborough House.

47   A wintery scene from the door of the Post Office showing the telephone and electric wires brought down by heavy icing. Some of the poles came down later during the hard winter of 1947.

48   A sketch of Norton Hall Farm by Mr P.G. Hunt, an artist and much respected Post Master, as seen from the entrance to his Post Office. This was drawn in 1937, during the first year of the twelve he spent there.

49 St. Aldhem's Roman Catholic Church completed at Bowden Hill in 1938. Some of the local wise men at that time queried the steepness of the site which had been chosen, besides which spring water seemed to be discharging there. Their fears were soon realized when one or two cracks appeared and the building was deemed unsafe. It was not until 1976 that this church was lowered, extended and modified to effect a neat and attractive appearance.

50 Some members of Chilcompton Brass Band led by Superintendent Jim Burge head the Chapel procession up Bowden Hill on Anniversary day c.1913. The two girls just right of centre are sisters Ruby, with basket, and Eleanor Padfield. In 1994 Ruby is the sole survivor of the large family of William and Sara Padfield. Behind the flags are blacksmith's premises where successive generations named Gait worked through the 19th century. The banner still survives at the Chapel and is in very good condition.

51 An early 1900's picture of Bowden Hill before the Cenotaph arrived. The house on the right was demolished to make more room for St. Aldhelm's Church. The fields behind were smaller in those days.

52 The unveiling and dedication of the War Memorial by the Bishop of Bath and Wells on 29.3.21. The seven choir members standing in a line are left to right (1) ?, (2) Mr Petit, (3) Cliff Bailey, (4) Ernest Sperring, (5) Ted Carpenter, (6) Harold Witcombe, (7) ?, Bill Emery is the choir man on the left of the umbrella. On a very wet day the photographer is to be commended on magnifying the background with such clarity, showing the blacksmith's shop, centre-foreground, and the houses in Britannia Yard, back left.

53 A 1960's picture which has changed little except for St. Aldhelm's Church on the right. The small dark building attached to it was erected here in 1911 and was extensively used as a R.C. Church, a Community Hall (billiards, whist drives, etc.) and a reading room.

PTE. J. TAPP, SOM. L.I.   L?N, GLOS. REG?
GUN? S. BURGE, R.F.A.   ?EIN CANADIAN "
  " C.R. VEASEY. "   ??SKINS, R.E.
P?A.M. DE STE CROIX ? ?   ??SKINS, STAFFA C?
PTE. C. PALE, RIFLE ??   ??HKINS, ?? ?

OCR?   ?ORD
A. EM?   ??
THEY   ?E. "

54 A wreath in the shape of an anchor placed on the cenotaph by Lieutenant R.H.C. Heptinstall captain of HMS Chilcompton on Saturday 7th July 1962 on behalf of the officers and ship's company. These were entertained during the day by members of the Parish Council and events included a tour of the village, a sumptious lunch at the Railway Inn, a cricket match, tea at the Britannia Inn, and skittles, darts and supper at the Redan Inn.

55 A mid-19th century picture of Anne Catherine Hippisley at Fry's Well. 1994 heralds the bi-centenary of Coleridge's visit and poem. (246 MTC)

Downside Lodge.

56 Downside Lodge and stables before demolition to make way for Downside Close.

57 Part of Wells Road in the early 1920's. The detached house is where a barrage balloon crashed on the roof during World War 2 (MTC 234). The house was built by Arthur Bradbury in 1916 at a cost of £294.14s.8½d and for a long time was the home of much respected Bert Webber and his wife Joyce. Arthur also built 'Sunnyside' along the road. Notice the paraffin lamp which was one of nine illuminating the roads of Chilcompton from 1910 to 1930 when electricity arrived. The building back left of the lamp was the Bennell Bakery Premises.

58 Part of Stockhill Road as on 7.3.1942. The car on the left is a 1934 Singer 10 and is parked outside the home of its owner Mr Skinner. In 1974 an entrance was made there when "Greenways", a bungalow estate for the elderly, was built on the extensive gardens behind these houses. The nearer car might look like a Wolseley but is a 12hp Rover.

59 Up to 1925 a tall beach tree (see No. 75 in Focus One) stood at the corner where the Co-op now stands and it was a meeting point for the "chaps of the village". The picture shows some of the two families of Sheppards plus two cousins playing see-saw on what was left of the beech tree. The Co-op is being built in the background. Left to right Eric, Lucy, Rex Crouch (cousin), Len, Mary, Charlie, David, Reg, Dennis Crouch and Bill.

60 This c.1940 Co-op picture features the staff minus Alec Pitman who had been called into his butcher's department (left).

61   A close-up of the group plus Alec. Left to right Ted Turner, Reg Lockyear, Charlie Gregory (manager), Sybil Ashman, Alec Pitman, Ken Scott and Jack Scott.

49

The Saw Mill

62 Just across the road from the Co-op front was the access road to the Railway Station and the south entrance to Sheppards Saw Mill. This picture, taken from that entrance, shows work sheds and the 90ft Jib Butters Crane just before the Mill closed on 31.8.1984.

63 A view from the other side of the crane. Some of the Saw Mill's history is on page 46 MTC.

64 Albert Dennett and Reg Nash standing by a very large Black Italian Poplar which was taken from the sawmill yard to Lydney in 1940 for the manufacture of plywood for use in the war effort.

65 A group at the Sawmill during 1939. Left to right—Top row—(1) Reg Nash, (2) Stan Pike, (3) Mick Padfield, (4) Vern Stuckey. Middle row—(1) Jack Croker, (2) Jim Chivers, (3) Eric Sheppard, (4) Gilb Perkins. Front row—(1) Bill Creed, (2) Len Bailey, (3) Albert Bailey.

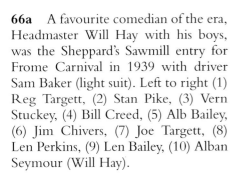

66a A favourite comedian of the era, Headmaster Will Hay with his boys, was the Sheppard's Sawmill entry for Frome Carnival in 1939 with driver Sam Baker (light suit). Left to right (1) Reg Targett, (2) Stan Pike, (3) Vern Stuckey, (4) Bill Creed, (5) Alb Bailey, (6) Jim Chivers, (7) Joe Targett, (8) Len Perkins, (9) Len Bailey, (10) Alban Seymour (Will Hay).

Water Mills

66b This is all that was left of Padfield's Mill in the lower part of the valley near Somer House in the 1950's. The Mill was used by James Padfield as a base for making edge tools from 1840 to 1899 although records of 1866 and 1872 give David Padfield as proprietor. James was one of several generations of Padfield's who worked their forges for at least 100 years, and he lived in a terraced house at the rear of Britannia Yard. His work there was continued by his son William who moved to Brook House in 1899 where he worked two forges and exported some of his tools as far afield as Russia. In 1902 he moved again to new premises in Baker's Lane now called Bevois House. One of his 10 children, Curtis, (A.C. Padfield), continued the business.

66c The mill house in middle of the valley (106 MTC) with adjacent watercress beds. The bed nearest the mill has as its border the foundations of Werret's House (81 MTC). Picture taken from the South West.

Mostly Family Groups

67 Mrs Clara Hodges with children. Left to right Ellen, Annie, baby Charles, and Lucy, taken c.1890.

68 Mrs Clara Hodges again with her husband William c.1901. Left to right— Rear— Bill, Ellen, Annie, Lucy and Charlie. Front—Eudie and Hugh. Pictured at their home, Norton Hall Farm, Bowden Hill. William died a few years after this picture was taken on 19.4.1905. Son Charlie died 5.2.1970 aged 82.

69 Lucy Hodges c.1908 when employed in the Arthur Waugh household at West Hampstead pictured with a little boy who was destined to become a famous novelist – Evelyn Arthur St. John Waugh (1903–66). Lucy married James Sheppard and her sister Annie married his brother John (Jack).

70 A 1927 picture of Miss Ellen Hodges with some of her nephews and nieces—all Sheppards. Rear left to right—Ellen, David, Bill, Reg, Tom. Front—Eric, Winnie, Mary, Charlie. Winnie died of TB aged 16.

71 Mrs Annie Sheppard with two of her children Winnie and Len c.1916.

72 Jim and Lucy Sheppard with their daughter Muriel, in front and sons Charlie, Tom, Bill, Eric and David. Jim was the founder of the Sawmill.

73 Another picture of the Targett family which featured in Focus One 39 and 40. The occasion was George and Elizabeth's Golden Wedding celebration in April 1950 and again their 12 children were present together with grandchildren and great-grandchildren. This was taken at the rear of Church House (which several of them had helped to build) with the scouts hut in the background.

Rear group, left to right—(1) Jack Targett, (2) Leslie Hiscocks, (3) Mary Targett, (4) Graham Targett (child), (5) David Targett (Jim), (6) Leslie Obern, (7) Dennis Obern, (8) Raymond Obern, (9) Evelyn Targett, (10) David Targett, (11) Grace Wood, (12) Tom Targett, (13) Gerald Targett, (14) Leonard Targett, (15) Eric Obern (boy), (16) Derek Targett (child), (17) Fred Targett.

Front row—(1) David Obern, (2) Valerie Obern, (3) Edie White, (4) Sandra White (baby), (5) George Targett (junior) (Harry), (6) Elizabeth Targett, (7) George Targett (senior), (8) Ellen Hiscocks (Nell), (9) John Hiscocks, (10) Win Obern, (11) Cynthia Targett.

74 Another family which proliferated during the 1920's and 30's was the Colbourne's of Wells Road beginning with Herbert, and his wife Elizabeth who had come from a family of 21 Joneses at Stratton.

75 Posing in the grounds of the old Miner's Welfare Hall at Wells Road with their parents are the 13 Colbourne children at Joan's Wedding. Left to right, numbers denote seniority—Back row—David (1), Christopher (6), Robert (3). Middle row—Leo (7), Agnes (5), Pauline (11), Joan (2), Margaret (9), Laurence (12). Front row—Gertrude (8), Mary (4), Herbert (dad), Elizabeth (mum), Clare (13), Lucy (10).

76   A photo taken of a family 'get together' c.1962 at the hall features most of the Colbourne offspring.

77 A 1903 picture of the Parsonage Lane shoemaker and cobbler William Carpenter and his wife Lucy, neé Blacker, holding baby Ida who later became John Sheppard's second wife. Father William is holding Mary who married Maurice Payne of Chewton Mendip. In between is Jim who married Melita Walter and, middle front, is Annie who married Ed Wilkins. Baby Caroline (Carrie) arrived in 1906 and eventually married Reg Obern.

78 Mrs Martha Carver whose husband and 4 sons appear on the next picture. She also had 7 or 8 daughters, 4 of whom were Augusta, Alice, Lisa, and Caroline.

79 Father Fred sitting next to youngest son Jack. Standing are sons George, Fred and Jim. c.1917.

80 Fred Carver (in uniform) on the previous picture married Eleanor (Nelly) Horler and these are their 11 children. Left to right with numbers denoting seniority—Adrian (9), Philip (8), Glyn (11), Cecil (4), Eleanor (Lana) (6), Duncan (7), Francis (Jim) (3), Brian (1), Basil (10), Colin (5), and John (2). Taken in 1976 at Highfield Crescent.

81 Joe Pearce in the 1890's when he was living in the little cottage which faces north and is attached to Bowden Hill House. He was a taxidermist and was related to the following Gould and Davis families. One brother William became the village butcher and another, Jim, was a carpenter living in Hillbro next to the Chapel in Baker's Lane.

82 Frank Gould complete with violin.

83 Tom Gould pictured with his sister Freda on his 21st birthday.

84 Freda Gould married Tom Davis and they had 11 children, 10 of whom are featured here with them. Left to right, numbers denote seniority—Ray (3), Mabel (1), Len (4), Irene (6), Ivor (7), Jim (2), Mary (11), Edgar (5), Alan (10), and Trevor (9), missing is Rex (8) but he is featured on picture 98.

85 The six children of Bertram Veale—the back three by a first marriage and the three in front from a second marriage to Anne Whittock of Chewton Mendip. All six were born along Wells Road. Rear left to right —Clifford, Marion, Reg. Front—Beatrice, Phyllis, Ivan.

86 Edward Clarke preparing the frame for the "Great Bede" bell at Downside Abbey in 1905. The Bell was named in memory of Dom Roger Bede Vaughan OSB., an old boy of Downside, who became the second Archbishop of Sydney, Australia. He was born on the 9th January 1834 and died 19th August 1883.

87 This is Leonard Dunford with his son Eric on Parsonage Lane during a time of snow. Len worked in the office at the Saw Mill and was Parish Council Clerk for a number of years. He married Edward Clarke's daughter Ruth.

88 Leonard and Ruth Dunford's children pictured at the same place in the same sequence as their 1954 picture in Focus One (65). Behind them the Britannia Yard has changed beyond all recognition. Their names are Jack, Margaret, Leslie and Eric and the occasion for their re-union was the funeral of their beloved mother Ruth on 21.5.91. Their father died in 1963 aged 60.

Individuals

89   A clear picture of Thomas Bevan, a cobbler, who lived at The Wingles and was featured in picture 51 of Focus One.

90 A nice picture of Sara Jane Parker taken in 1884 when she was 21. She married Chilcompton edge-toolmaker William Curtis Padfield the same year and they had 10 children.

91 An early picture of Chilcompton Police Constable Henry William Noble who lived in 2 Hollway Cottages and was the grandfather of Nora Burge of Fry's Well. (See 'Interesting Letters').

92a A colourful character during the first half of the 1900's was Theothilus (Alf) Ponting. At different times he was a farm worker, and butcher besides which he was favoured with a good veterinary knowledge. A big man with a nice sense of humour, he was born at Shell House Farm and also lived at Greenditch Farm Cottage, Three Tuns, Bowden Hill House, and two different houses at Wells Road before ending his days aged 87 at his former shop at the foot of Norton Down Lane.

92b Mr Samuel Taylor of Bennell Batch on his 100th birthday. Believed to be the oldest surviving Coldstream Guardsman, he was accorded a musical tribute by drummers from the Coldstream, Irish, Grenadier, and Scots Guards regiments on 15th February 1991. He died later that year.

Pictures of Village Interest

93 Harriet and Herbert James (Bert) Golledge with infant son George.

93a Harriet Golledge with daughter Caroline and son George outside their home at Rookery Farm c.1932. A few years later Bert, in the previous picture, built a new farmhouse on the right where the gate is. The old house is still used as a store-cum-cattle shed (MTC 104).

93b A c.1926 picture of a 1923 Bean car made in Wolverhampton with proud owner Bert Golledge. In the car is daughter Caroline, wife Harriet, niece Marian Marshall, and son George at the wheel. George followed in his father's footsteps and became a pillar of strength to St. John's Church, the Parish Council, and Chilcompton in general. George's wife Josephine was also treasurer and a tireless worker for St. John's. It was a big loss to the village when they emigrated to Canada on 14.4.94.

94 George Golledge standing on part of his extensive Water Cress beds in Chilcompton Valley c.1956. This was one of the very few occasions when the beds froze over because normally the tepid spring water from two springs 50 metres away would remedy this. The lane from upper Baker's Lane to the Valley (upper left) was one of the five tracks which led to the Mill.

95 A distant 1930's view of the same watercress beds taken from the railway station looking north with part of the Mill House roof visible. Barely discernable in the fore-ground are Bert Golledge and George Durrant.

96 Cutting cress in 1931—George Golledge, George Durrant and Bert Golledge.

97 George Golledge lived at Rookery Farm for many years while still cultivating his watercress and this is a 1953 photo of Marie, one of his four daughters, helping with the milking.

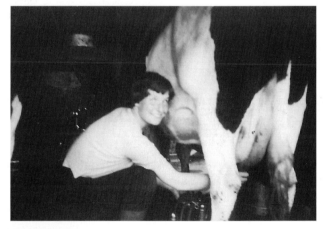

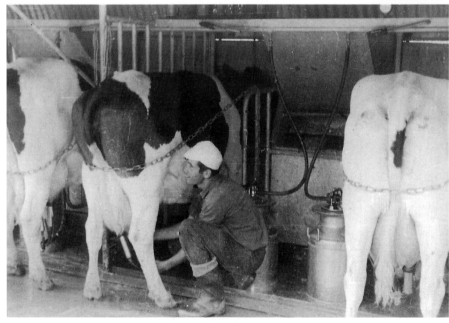

98 Rex Davis busy at the milking process in 1950 at Rookery Farm.

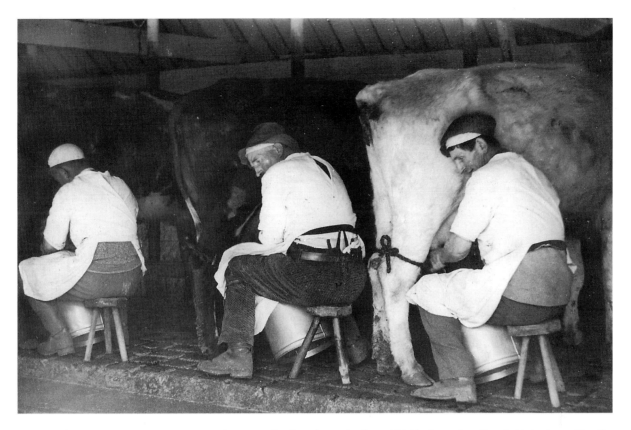

99 Milking time at Manor Farm, this time by hand, in the late 1930's featuring Frank Pointing, Charlie Durrant and George Burge.

100 A scene of seed planting near Halfway Waters, with horses Prince and Jolly together with Frank Pointing, George Sugg and Reg Mattick who is wondering if he will ever finish. This picture was taken on the same day as No. 99.

102 Sam Baker again at the age of 9 and sister Josephine in choir dress at the Chapel door.

103 Village butchers Ernest Pearce and William, his father, with their delivery cart at the entrance to their house and shop called Orchardleigh in The Street. (See pages 54/55 MTC).

104 And here is the dreaded slaughterhouse which stood at the foot of Norton Down Lane on the rise opposite The Hollies. Dead animals everywhere and a bucket of blood. Unharmed are William and Herbert Pearce and their tea-lady Gladys Pike who is holding a chopper.

105 William Pearce again with a grandson standing near what is now the entrance to Somer Lea. His three sons, who helped with his butchery business, were (1) Herbert, (2) Leonard and (3) Ernest, named in seniority.

106   John Hoare (left) helping his friend Hugh Hodges build a hayrick.

106a   At the rear of Norton Hall Farm Hugh Hodges (left) poses with his sister Marie and close friend and neighbour Derek Hunt. This picture is remarkable because it shows hardworking Hugh nicely dressed.

106b   Another picture of the Hodges family at the same location (1) ?, (2) Dolly Hodges, (3) Clara Hodges, (4) Marie Hodges, (5) William Hodges.

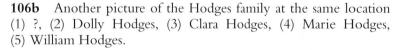

107   A quaint old picutre of a pony and gig again at the rear of Norton Hall Farm. The boy is Charlie Hodges with his sister Edie who is sitting in the gig. Charlie and Edie emigrated to Canada. Their father features in the next photo.

108   Another horse and trap picture this time taken outside the Manor House in Church Lane, Stratton-on-the-Fosse c.1900. Posing is William Hodges, (left) from Norton Hall Farm, who ran a 'taxi' business as well as a farm. The other occupant is probably a client.

109 A c.1915 picture taken outside the Railway Inn, now the Somerset Wagon, of Fred Perkins, driver and innkeeper; Rhoda Tapp, (left) who became "Nick" James; the little boy is Len Webber the son of the blacksmith whose tiled roof shop is just behind; and Fred's wife Nellie neé Tapp (Rhoda's sister). The main road (Broadway) can be been passing between the horse and the wall.

110 A c.1920 picture again at the Somerset Wagon features Arthur Perkins, Fred's father, with his granddaughter Brenda Perkins who later married Viv Cullen. Arthur, who married 3 times, left the Somerset Wagon to take over at the Bunch of Grapes Inn at Shepton Mallet. From there he went to the White Hart at Wells. Arthur's other son Harold took over the Bunch of Grapes later and then the Red Lion at Shepton Mallet. The car looks like a Model T Ford (tin lizzie).

'Charabanc' Outings

111 A c.1927 outing for members of Christ Church, Stockhill. Note the solid tyres and, lower left, speed 12 m.p.h. Note also that passengers sat five abreast with a separate door at the end of each row of seats. Standing left to right—(1) ?, (2) ?, (3) Alb Ridout, (4) ?, (5) Les Dowling, (6) ? (down), (7) Albie Heal (back), (8) ?, (9) Bill Gibbings, (10) Renie Hoskins, (11) Dorothy Moore (back), (12) ?, (13) Christine Llewellyn, (14) Jim Stacey, (15) Susan Coles, (16) Bert Gibbings. Driver ?. Seated left to right—(1) ?, (2) Jack Holland, (3) Charlie Heal, (4) Jim Coles, (5) ? (boy), (6) ?, (7) Henry Witcombe, (8) Gertie Bryant, (9) Mary Derrick, (10) Phyllis Gould, (11) Rev'd Thomas Upward, (12) Gwen Gibbings, (13) Sarah Moore, (14) Mrs Hoskins, (15) ?.

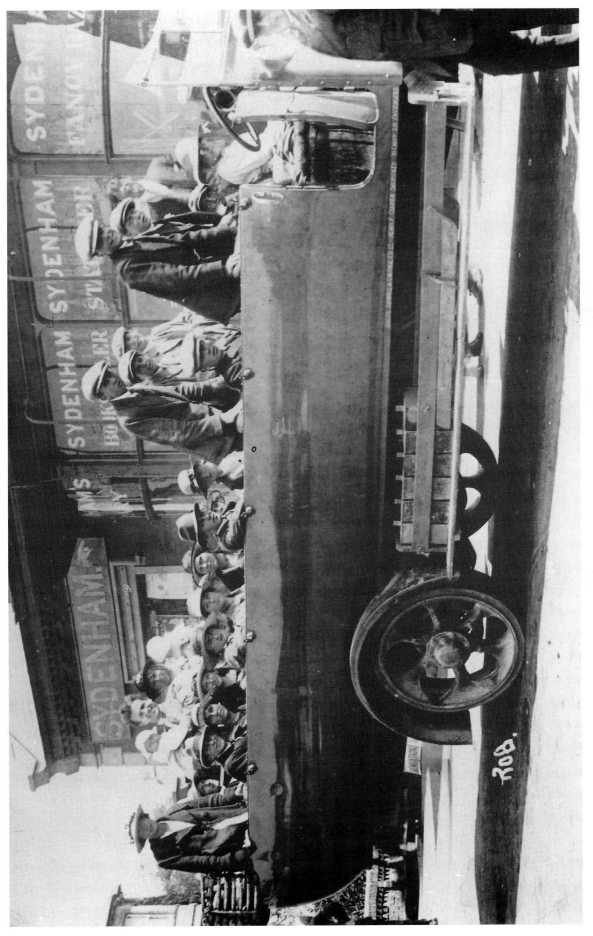

112 Outing to Bournemouth on 25.6.1921 probably by members of the Night-School Class of Chilcompton School. Note the large 'pram' hood stacked at the back ready to be passed hand over hand to the front at the slightest hint of rain. Writing on the side states Bristol Tramways and Carriage Co. Ltd. to carry 28 passengers. Standing left to right—(1) Ellen Targett, (2) Twin boy, Ian Mitchell Cox, (3) Sam Cox, (4) Sarah Jane Padfield, (5) Twin boy, Nigel Jason Cox, (6) Bill Veale, (7) Jim Bastable, (8) Fred Targett, (9) Tom Targett, (10) Dan Ball, (11) Fred Brown, (12) Driver ?. Seated left to right—(1) Edie Gould, (2) Ron Clarke, (3) Ruby Clarke, (4) Eleanor Padfield, (5) Vera Dunford, (6) Mary Carpenter, (7) Faye Carter, (8) Bill Bryant, (9) (part) Melita Walter, (10) Ida Carpenter, (11) Jim Coles (12) Harry Targett, (13) Dora Grace.

113 A c.1928 St John's Choir outing to Weston-super-Mare. Either the weather is inclement or its cold in those open buses.

```
      (1)      (4)          (7)                  (12)  (14)
        (2)      (5)        (9)      (10)         (13)
          (3)      (6)      (8)          (11)          (15)
```

Top group in coach—(1) ?, (2) ?, (3) Bob Sugg, (4) Curt Padfield, (5) Gladwys Burge, (6) Frank Pointing, (7) Reg Beck, (8) Dick Holder, (9) Eddie Bevan, (10) George Golledge, (11) Alice Targett, (12) Ron Beck, (13) Caroline Golledge, (14) Grace Targett, (15) Frank Eyles (Driver).

```
                                      (18)
                          (11)
      (3)          (6)          (13)      (17)      (21)                              (28)
    (2)      (5)        (8)  (9)        (15)      (20)    (22)(23) (24) (25)(26)
  (1)      (4)        (7)    (10) (12) (14) (16) (19)                          (27)
```

Group below the coach—(1)Charlie Lye, (2) Baldwin Bailey, (3) Len Kerton, (4) Len Bailey, (5) Ken Mattick, (6) Archie Bailey, (7) Charlie Bailey (below), (8) Harriet Golledge, (9) Vera Mogg, (10) Reitha Sugg, (11) Bert Golledge, (12) Vera Baker, (13) Sarah Golledge, (14) Grace Burge, (15) Edith Bailey, (16) Mick Padfield, (17) Ted Bailey, (18) Elsie Burge, (19) Harry Bevan, (20) Irma Sperring, (21) Ernest Sperring, (22) Ann Baker, (23) Connie Watts, (24) Bertie Watts, (25) ?, (26) Ruby Lovell, (27) Rose Mogg, (28) Edwin Carpenter.

114 A possible Mothers Union outing to Weymouth c.1928. Standing—(1) Dorothy Flagg, (2) Moira Flagg (baby), (3) Bessie Knowles, (4) Alice Mogg, (5) Maria Shearn, (6) Sarah (Sally) Moore, (7) Mrs Arthur Perkins. Seated—(1) Clem Jones (driver), (2) Mrs Wilmot, (3) Daisy Witcombe, (4) Gladys Dando, (5) ?, (6) Gladys Bryant, (7) Lily Coles, (8) Alice Llewellyn, (9) Elsie Burge, (10) Minnie Coles (11) Susan Coles.

115 Off to Cheddar in a coach owned by Shearn Bros of Midsomer Norton are possibly members and supporters of the Cresswell Girls Club. Back Standing—(1)Nick James, (2) Vera Dunford, (3) ?, (4) Madge Sperring, (5) May Smith (back), (6) Edith Gould, (7) Mother and baby, (8) Mabel Dunford (back), (9) Alice Llewellyn, (10) Annie Llewellyn, (11) Annie's child, (12) Lily Coles, (13) Minnie Coles, (14) Faye Carter, (15) (up) Miriam (Dolly) Dunford, (16) Margery Dunford, (17) Evelyn Brown, (18) Rose Dowling. Seated—(1) ?, (2) Christine Llewellyn, (3) Suzy Coles, (4) ?, (5) Lily Flower, (6) Elsie Wheeler, (7) Dorothy Moore, (8) Sarah Moore (nose and mouth only), (9) Ethel Obern, (10) Annie Padfield, (11) ?, (12) Driver, (13) Blanche Arthurs.

116 A group pictured at Weston-super-Mare on the 1928 St. John's Choir Outing. (1) Jim Bevan, (2) Curt Padfield, (3) Jack Stuckey, (4) Charlie Bailey, (5) Frank Coles, (6) George Golledge, (7) Bert Golledge, (8) Albert Stuckey, (9) Caroline Golledge, (10) Marion Marshall, (11) Harriet Golledge, (12) Baldwin (Bunny) Bailey.

117 On another choir outing these have mysteriously become separated from the main group to form their own quartet on Weston-super-Mare pier. George Golledge, Reg Targett, Gwen Pike and Vera Baker. In 1994 George has just emigrated to Canada, Reg is in Bath, Gwen is now Mrs Camden and lives in New Zealand, and Vera is Mrs Harris in America. George is wearing his school cap — Midsomer Norton Grammar School, now Norton Hill School. It was navy with mid-blue bands and the badge was the Somerset dragon.

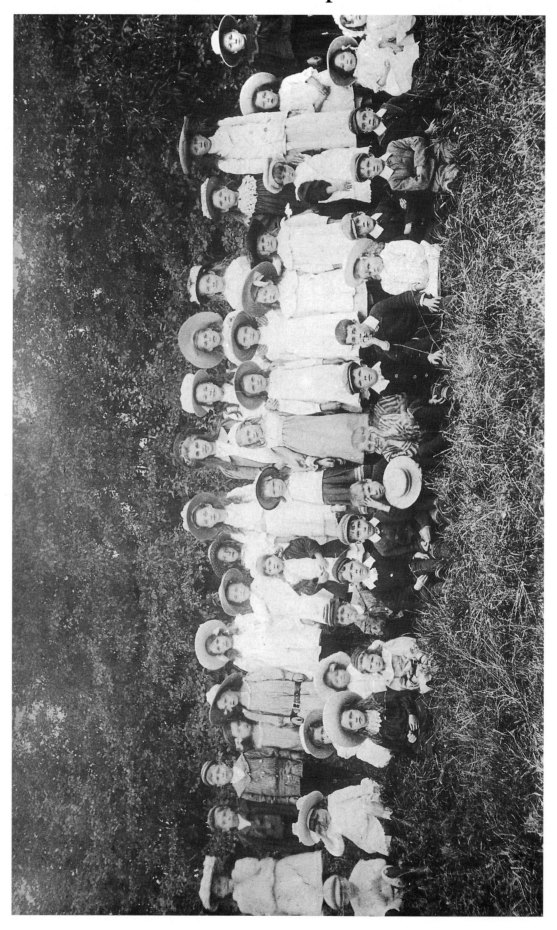

118 An early c.1913 group all in Sunday best — tea party at the Vicarage perhaps. Only a few names here. Back row—(5) Ida Carpenter, (6) Eva Singer, (9) Mary Carpenter, (11) Ellis Burge, (16) Olive Eyles, (17) Jessie Hillier. Second row—(2) Carrie Carpenter, (4) Doris Burge, (5) Annie Carpenter. Seated—(8) Bill Veale, (12) Harry Veale, (18) Dora Holder.

119 A possible quarterly circuit meeting c.1914 tea party at Spring View, Fry's Well for the Methodist Chapel. Left to right—(1) Rev'd Payne, (2) John Small, (3) ?, (4) ?, (5) ?, (6) James Sheppard, (7) William Challenger, (8) Rev'd Naylor, (9) Isaac Moore, (10) Susan Challenger, (11) Lucy Moore, (12) Gertrude Challenger.

120 Mothers Union members in the garden of Somer House, Britannia Close, pictured at the farewell party to honour Mrs Francis Greenway. Back six—Peggy Merrilees, Dot Brown, Marjorie Jackson, Susan Gibbings, Hilda Bailey, Mildred Wood. Middle four—Elsie Shipton, Frances Greenway, Minnie Knowles, Hilda Noel. Front—Ethel Smith.

121 Happy faces on a Womens Institute outing to Bournemouth in the 1960's. Left to right—Gwen Moore, Dorothy Hillard, Doris Findell, Betty Maidment, Beatrice Kirtland, Alice Targett, Win Burge, Ruth Dunford, Kath Wadman.

122 The hard-working ladies at Bill Freeman's rug and carpet-making establishment at Shell House pause for a photo in c.1946.

Left to right—(1) Enid Stevens, (2) Mildred Gumbleton, (3) Mabel Welsford, (4) Kathleen Shaw, (5) Patricia Carver, (6) Mrs Lord, (7) Jean Draper, (8) Mary Perkins, (9) Max Symes, (10) Elsie Lovell, (11) Audrey Lovell, (12) Keith Freeman, (13) Eileen Lovell, (14) Muriel Heal, (15) Margaret Cornick, (16) Joan Green.

123 A 1950's Senior Citizens Christmas party in the old village hall. Standing—Beatrice (Maud) Matthews, Margaret Stephens, Cecil Hiscox, Stan Charlton, Fred Coles. Seated—Lesley Craig, Winifred Bishop, Beatrice Moon, Barlow Moon, Charlie Bishop.

124 A picture taken at the side of the Co-op car park of members of Chilcompton Royal British Legion en-route to the War Memorial for the Remembrance Day Service c. 1960. (1) Stan Charlton–standard bearer, (2) Fred Hale, First Three: (1) Jim Moore, (2) Bill Denning, (3) Arthur Dunford, Second Three: (1) Cyril Burge, (2) Rev'd Robert Turnbull, (3) Cliff Perkins. Among those behind are Len Dunford, Tom Cook, George Golledge, Wally Moon, Bill Sheppard, Jim Moore, and Bert Strawbridge.

125 Mr Fred Clarke plants a tree at Bowden Hill in 1974 to commemorate his retirement after 15 years as Parish and District Councillor. His fellow councillors suggested this as he was much respected for spending countless hours on Chilcompton's behalf even though he worked long hours as a self-employed nurseryman. Left to right—Doug Chivers, Bert Webber, John Lewis, Joan Strawbridge, Wallace Moon, John Pilgrim (top of head), Bert Monckton, Alban Seymour, Clifford Perkins, Grahame Pickford, Jim Painting.

126 St John's Sunday School Group c. 1965 when average attendance was 50 to 60 pictured in Shell House yard. Front seated left to right—(1) Lauren Strawbridge, (2) Bryony Strawbridge, (3) Lorraine Hoare, (4) ?, (5) Christopher Curtis, (6) Annette Davis, (7) Christopher Veale, (8) Caroline Clarke. Second row (double)—(1) Teresa Hawtin, (2) Pauline Davis, (3) Tina Hawtin, (4) ?, (5) Janice Purnell, (6) Michael Evans, (7) Cindy Matthews, (8) Tim Curtis, (9) Priscilla Pain, (10) Gene Pain (forward), (11) Alan Hartley (rear), (12) Nigel Dando, (13) Phillip Chivers, (14) Timothy Heymann, (15) Paul Mattick, (16) Nigel Clarke, (17) Nigel Wood, (18) Cheryl Strawbridge (forward), (19) Brian Evans. Third Row—(1) Lorraine Latchem, (2) Ivy Gullick, (3) David Wilcox, (4) Hilary de Costobadie, (5) Anne Dunford, (6) Bronwen Hartley, (7) Joanna Hartley, (8) Randy Welsford, (9) Celia Horler, (10) Kathy Horler (forward), (11) Winnifred Whittington, (12) Elizabeth Adnett. Back row—(1) Josie Hawtin, (2) Carol Evans, (3) Johanna Dando, (4) Adrian Wood, (5) Roger Wilcox, (6) Robert Hartley, (7) Mark Strawbridge, (8) Keith Horler, (9) Malcolm Moore.

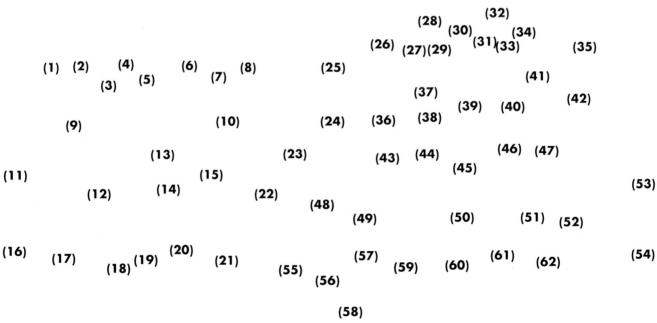

127 A Sunday School Christmas Party at the Church House in 1947.—(1) Ann Bowen, (2) Duncan Carver, (3) Robert Hembry, (4) Michael Perry, (5) David Gullick, (6) Carlton Margary, (7) Ray Chivers, (8) Pat Hembry, (9) Reg Horler, (10) Colin Carver, (11) Adrian Beck, (12) Bill Quinn, (13) Melvyn Bowen, (14) Pat Quinn, (15) Gillian Kiddle, (16) Lana Carver, (17) Philip Carver, (18) Adrian Carver, (19) Muriel Box, (20) John Gumbleton, (21) Michael Monk, (22) Mary Monk, (23) John Quinn, (24) Brian Morris, (25) Bill Eyles, (26) David Strawbridge, (27) Betty Horler, (28) Gordon Curtis, (29) Sheila Curtis, (30) Ivy Kiddle, (31) Evan Burge, (32) Jim Carver, (33) Shirley Cox, (34) David Padfield, (35) Derek Webster (36) Sally Brown, (37) Eileen Hobbs, (38) ?, (39) Margaret Horler, (40) David Beck, (41) Robert Beck, (42) ?, (43) Mary Prior, (44) Malcolm Curtis, (45) Irene Jones, (46) Dianne Freeman, (47) Reg Horler, (48) ?, (49) ?, (50) Dianne Chivers, (51) Keith Freeman, (52) Alice Padfield, (53) Paddy Lane, (54) Barbara Box, (55) Fred Lane, (56) Paddy Lane, (57) Ann Chilcott, (58) Rev'd Ernest Hill, (59) Margaret Kiddle, (60) Lesley Dunford, (61) Brian Pike. (62) Joyce Holder.

Guides and Brownies

128 Some of the Chilcompton Guides at an annual camp under canvas at Minehead in the 1930's. Back four—(1) Margaret Eyles, (2) Grace Burge, (3) Evelyn Targett, (4) Maud Kerton. Front four—(1) ?, (2) Ruth Dunford (leader), (3) Angel Padfield, (4) Ciss Gumbleton.

128a Camp fire barbeque at Guide Camp c. 1928. Left to right—(1) Gladwys Burge, (2) Vera Baker, (3) ? (rear), (4) Bertha Burge, (5) Frampton (rear), (6) Mary Targett, (7) Rose Mogg, (8) Ciss Fuller.

129 A Group of Brownies with their leader Brown Owl Miss Christine Mattick c. 1940. Back four—Phyllis Chivers, Joyce Horler, Muriel Curtis, Jean Curtis. Middle three—Barbara Beck, Ann Berry, Joan Gould. Front three—Bernice Gullick, Margaret Beck, Brenda Smith.

130 Guides and Brownies pictured at the Chapel Hall around 1965. Front nine sitting left to right—(1) Yvonne Stuckey, (2) Mary Jones, (3) Julie Matthews, (4) Vivien Bailey, (5) Tina Hawtin, (6) Teresa Hawtin, (7) Cheryl Strawbridge, (8) Claire Wellington, (9) Linda Sobey. Second row kneeling—(1) Priscilla Pain, (2) Maxine Barnes, (3) Judith Reakes, (4) Sarah Wellington, (5) Kay Dando, (6) Johanna Dando, (7) Caroline West, (8) Jacqueline Sheppard, (9) Judith Eyles, (10) Carol Evans. Eight in the third row—(1) Josie Hawtin, (2) Helen Geach, (3) Kay Wellington, (4) Ruth Guilliford, (5) Judith Crockett, (6) Avril Hiscox, (7) Rachael Sheppard, (8) Mary Turner. Eight at the rear—(1) ?, (2) Josephine Turner, (3) ?, (4) Barbara Bailey, (5) Ann Bailey, (6) Sandra Stuckey, (7) June Maidment, (8) Christine Sobey.

130a Brownie Guides of the Chilcompton Pack with the District Commissioner, Miss M. Foster, looking at their new handbooks at an open evening in April 1968 at the village hall. Back row—(1) Judith Eyles, (2) Caroline West, (3) Pat Davis, (4) Sarah Wellington, (5) Priscilla Pain, (6) Helen Geach. Middle row—(1) Teresa Hawtin, (2) Jane Bryant, (3) Cheryl Strawbridge, (4) ?, (5) ?, (6) Kay Dando, (7) Vivien Bailey. Front row—(1) Susan Geach, (2) Jill Davis, (3) Claire Wellington, (4) Sally Ann Waite, (5) Commissioner Foster, (6) Judith Reakes, (7) Mary Jones, (8) Josephine Rich.

131 The Chilcompton Ladies Choir pictured at a concert they gave in March 1984. Back row—Vivienne Moon, Mary Langley, Rosemary Breddy, Jean Dimmick, Grace Wallen, Daphne Trippick, Jane Sutherland, Kate Causer, June Brooks. Front row—Gwen Moore, Jean Sims, Margaret Curtis, Win Clover, Lilian Huber (conductor), Ron Huber (accompanist), Grace Wood, Barbara Fowler, Audrey Strawbridge, Jill Young.

132 Four members of Chilcompton Brass Band in the 1930's. Back two—Archie Bailey, Jack Witcombe. Front two—Charlie Steeds, Ivan Tottle.

Sport

133 Chilcompton Football Club 1919–20 cup-winning team pictured near the Britannia Inn. Back five—(1) Harry James, (2) Bert Perkins, (3) Reg Richards, (4) Bill Heal, (5) Harry Pike. Nine in third row—(1) Art Veasey, (2) Jim Baker (Britannia Innkeeper), (3) Mr Gordon, (4) Walt Shearn, (5) Alfie Perkins, (6) Jack Pike, (7) Mr Heal, (8) Mr Vinnell, (9) Ern Knowles. Five sitting—(1) Bert Knowles, (2) Stan Parfitt, (3) Bill Padfield, (4) Bill Dally, (5) Bill Bryant. Two kneeling—(1) Fred (Chummy) Smith, (2) Stan Perkins. Proud Harry Pike has his hand on son Jack's shoulder.

99

133a In 1955 Chilcompton won the covetted Somerset Junior Football Cup and were invited to visit Belgium with over 20 other cup-winning teams from all over England. Chilcompton was one of only two teams to win against the foreign opposition in Ostend. The score was 6-2 with Edgar Gane scoring four goals. Here is the team and supporters prior to departure. Wilf Perkins (captain) had received the Junior Cup almost 25 years to the day his father had done likewise (1930). Left to right standing—(1) Edgar Gane, (2) Walter Gane, (3) John Perkins, (4) Audrey Gane, (5) Laurence Targett, (6) Ralph MacDonald, (7) Mary Charles, (8) Brenda Charles, (9) Ray Gregory, (10) Diana Young, (11) Graham Young, (12) Henry Charles, (13) Jack Nash, (14) ?, (15) John Andrews, (16) Alf Perkins, (17) Ada Perkins, (18) John Charles, (19) Betty Perkins, (20) Edie Shearn (back), (21) Maureen Davidge (girl), (22) Jack Holland, (23) Lily Davidge, (24) Alma Lock, (25) Albie Alford (driver), (26) George Davidge, Left to right six crouching—(1) Roy Dark, (2) Ron Davidge, (3) Harold Blacker, (4) Cliff Perkins, (5) John Veale, (6) Wilf Perkins (capt).

134 Another cup-winning side—The Britannia Inn dart team of the 1950's. Back four—Ted Evans, Mick Lane, John Earle, Dave Strawbridge. Front four—Tommy Hawtin, Grahame Young, Jack Golledge, Billy Obern (innkeeper).

134a Chilcompton Cricket Team on 7th July 1962 waiting to play against HMS Chilcompton. Back row standing—left to right—(1) Michael Fricker, (2) Jim Moore, (3) Evan Burge, (4) Bill Coombes, (5) Peter Padfield, (6) Rodney Uphill, (7) Terry Moore. Sitting—(1) Gordon Sheppard, (2) Michael Pike, (3) Keith Coombes, (4) Adrian Beck, (5) Jim Perkins. Other team members were Eric Symes and Eric Obern. Matches were played here on the field next to Highfield Crescent where Golledge Close Estate has since been built. Behind the team is a deep valley, then part of the railway station, and the rear of the Somerset Wagon Inn is upper right.

134b Pictured at the club room at the Railway Inn is the pub's cup-winning shove-halfpenny team of 1958–9. Left to right—Gerald Heal, Harry Stephens, Tommy Hawtin, Jim Derrick, Len Kerton, George Heal and Jack Durrant. Team member Norman Veale was missing (as usual). Jim Derrick was the innkeeper for a long time here and two of his brothers, George and Tom were landlords at the Fire Engine Inn and The Tuckers Grave Inn respectively.

135   Local train 34042 about to stop at Binegar after the climb from Chilcompton pulled by a Bullied Pacific.

136   Train passing over a viaduct at Emborough Quarry.

137   A train from Binegar having steamed through Emborough Quarry, (in the background), over the A37 road, and passed by Moorewood signal box, now nears Coalpit Lane bridge as it passes Moorewood Sidings. Coal was brought the 1½ miles from Moorewood Colliery on a 23" trolley line to fill these waiting trucks. This point was also the depot for local coal hauliers.

138 A photo taken from the same position as 137 but looking the other way. The double-headed train from Chilcompton has just passed under Coalpit Lane "humpback" bridge. Protruding from the trees, centre right, is a Court Hotel Chimney.

139 Chilcompton signal box with Highfield Crescent behind. The deep valley between the two is barely discernible. On the right is one of two water columns: the other is on 140.

139a Inside Chilcompton signal box is Bill Coombes (right) duty signalman, with a colleague.

140 A general view looking west of the Railway Station which also features the water tower (left) and the tiny exposed and unheated waiting room on the right. The railway line was very steep coming from the right—it then almost levelled out at the station and rose sharply again in the distance.

141 A closer view of the rear of the station waiting room many years later.

141a The station waiting room is almost obscured by the length of this passenger train. Sheppard's Saw Mill crane stands out and the mysterious building above the engine is the top of the station water tower.

142 With the Fry's Well/Bowden Hill area in the background a train heads towards the twin-bore tunnel and then to Midsomer Norton.

143 A c. 1928 photo of 7 local gangers (railway maintenance workers) and one dog at Ilett's tunnel. Left to right—Harry Walters, Frank Coles, Bill Southway, Bill Prior, Jack Foxwell, Dick Symes and Sam Tucker. Jack Foxwell was killed by a train in 1951 at the other end of the left tunnel one foggy morning.

Moorewood Colliery

144 Page 222 in M.T.C. shows the coal trolley line leading from Stockhill top down to Moorewood Colliery. This picture features the line in reverse.

145 This later photo from the same position as 144 gives little indication that a line ever existed.

146 Moorewood winding engine house, having been unused since the colliery's first closure in 1876, is about to be brought into use again in 1909.

OLD PIT MOOREWOOD
(1)

147   Work commences in 1909 on the east end.

149   The erection of headgear in progress.

148   Work on the south side includes a surround for two Lancashire boilers and a base for the chimney stack.

150   The boilers are installed and the colliery is ready for production again. The shaft had originally been sunk in 1830 and coal was mined until 1876. This 1909 re-opening provided work for an average of 150 men until its final closure on 31.12.1932. See MTC 126

151   The owners and foremen pose after an inspection in the early 1920's.

152   Workmen sawing pit props.

153   Moorewood Colliery Rescue Brigade—Left to right—H. Gould, J. Rich, E. Ashley, B. Veale, A. Emery with Sergeant Instructor W. Riley.

154 In the colliery precincts there was a brickworks, pictured here, which incorporated a clay pit, 3 kilns, a cooling bay and a chimney.

155 After standing forlorn and idle for 40 years the brick chimney is blown up in 1973. A picture taken just prior to the explosion is No. 147 in Focus One.

156 200 metres east of the colliery was The Fire Engine Inn, a favoured and convenient meeting place for the miners, and this is now a private house.

Chilcompton in Wartime 1939–45

157 The local Home Guard Battalion in 1942 at Downside School (Stratton) sports grounds where training took place. The contingent consisted mainly of men from Chilcompton, Stratton, Holcombe, Coleford and Oakhill. It would be impossible to name individually the c250 men pictured here but hopefully many readers will be able to pick out a husband, father or relative. The front leader is Captain Hillier. Behind is—left to right—(1) John Moore (Hol), (2) ?, (3) ?, (4) Capt Charlie James (Chil), (5) 2nd Lieut Harry Durbin (Chil), (6) Dr Finn (Oakhill), (7) ?, (8) Bennett Greenway (Hol), (9) ?, (10) ?, (11) Mr Fry (Dentist). The tall figure of Arthur Box (Chil) stands out in the 4th full line from the left, 7th back. Capt Hillier was later killed in an accident with a hand grenade on the Rifle Range at Cockhill Quarry.

111

158 The Chilcompton Fire Brigade was stationed at Bowden Hill near the Post Office and for most of the war years it was manned from 6pm to 6am by one of five crews of four men each, all from the village. Two crews pictured here outside the "Fire Station" are left to right—Chief Fire Officer Bill Challenger, Alan Witcombe, Charlie Sheppard, Walt Fricker, Ern Flower, Fred Targett, Jim Coles and Gilb Perkins. Among others in the Brigade were Fred Vinnell, A. Perrett, leading fireman Bert Webber, Percy Hunt, Alan Wilcox, David Sheppard, Jim Targett, Fred Vinnell and Bob Sugg. Shepton Mallet Fire Brigade took responsibility during 6am to 6pm.

158b A close-up of the same group as 158—Ern Flower, Bill Challenger, Charlie Sheppard, Gilb Perkins, Jim Coles, Fred Targett, Walt Fricker and Alan Witcombe.

159 Bert and Ada Perkins from Bowden Hill, with one of their three sons, Arthur, (they also had 8 daughters) pictured at Buckingham Palace. Arthur is holding the Distinguished Service Medal he was awarded for his bravery on HMS Norfolk (heavy cruiser) during the engagement with the German battlecruiser Scharnhorst on Boxing Day 1943. He was also involved in the sinking of the battleship Bismark on 26/27 May 1941 and went on 14 dangerous convoys to Russia. During one of those trips 24 ships out of 28 were lost. Arthur was a popular lad in the village and was one of the first to volunteer for the Navy at the outbreak of the war when he was 19.

160 Hopefully they took the little boy off this bonfire before lighting it to celebrate the end of the war with Japan—V.J. Day 14th August 1945. After nearly 6 years of fighting this was the end and Chilcompton celebrated along with the rest of the country. A few months earlier on 8 May, another bonfire had been lit in this same place—Britannia Yard, to signal V.E. Day (Victory in Europe) and festivities had continued well into the night. Notice the standpipe against the wall which served most of the 12 houses in the yard with water.

Emborough

161 An aerial picture taken in July 1992 of The Court Hotel which has the postal address of Emborough but is in Chilcompton Parish. A large conservatory has since been added this side. The adjacent lodge and barn are on the right. Thickthorn Lane is further right and the main B3139 road is passing by. The S & D railway line emerged from the field centre right to pass under the road, through an embankment, and left the picture approximately bottom centre (138 Focus One), In the shrubbery, this side of the road, where a telegraph pole sticks out, there is a 1941 wartime pill box. Also the brown marks bottom right of the shrubbery is a geological find called a 'slipped strata' (MTC 34).

161a The other side of the Hotel showing the entrance door. Now called simply 'The Court' it is a very popular country hotel with a restaurant seating 60 and 12 guest rooms all ensuite. Further extensions are envisaged. When it was built c. 1800 it was called Lynch House by the owner, a Mr Smith, who was quite wealthy and his servants were housed in the basement rooms which are now used as cellars. The House was later called Lynch Hill House and titles since have been Lynchill Guest House, The Court Guest House, and The Court Hotel. It was always referred to as The Thousand Pound House by Downside schoolboys on their way to skate at Emborough Pond. The name Lynch is authentic enough (MTC34) and it would have been a suitable position for hangings, on high ground at the boundary of a village. The large Turkey Oak standing near the North Door is rumoured to be a hanging tree and a tall stone nearby is looked upon as a memorial but there is no evidence of the house being used as a Court. The lodge to the east of the Hotel was built from the rubble of a house which stood on the other side of the lane and which was demolished in 1874 to make way for the railway. The lodge was connected to the main house by an underground tunnel. A new west wing was built on the house in the 1960's. Other owners of the hotel have been wealthy William Ashman Green until c. 1870, stone mason John Chivers with wife Frances and eight children 1881, Alfred Whitehouse 1894 (Paymaster General-in-Chief R.N.), also Louis B. Beachamp 1899, James Morgan 1902, Arthur Campbell 1906, Edward Gould 1919, and Frederick Knight 1927. Later owners include Messrs. Crocker, Garstang, Nussbaum, Fox and Hayes. It was refurbished then reopened on 10.3.92 by present owners Sue Collins, Andrew Lamb and Malcolm Curtis. The once-important water well is now under the east end of the corridor of the west wing.

162   Jim Peppard (Sen), pictured with his horse, lived here along Coalpit Lane in very humble surroundings but was much respected locally. He also featured in Focus One 46, 57 and 161.

163   The turnpike cottage at Old Down in the 1950's. Sadly, the old windows have since been replaced with a modern type. This turnpike cottage was built in 1835 to control the coal traffic emerging from Coalpit Lane just opposite. It replaced the tollhouse which had been at the old parish boundary at lower Lynch Hill since 1767.

164 In the once large field behind the turnpike cottage stood a brickworks which has completely disappeared leaving pockets and undulations as the only clues. It was called the "Somerset Pipe, Tile & Brickworks" and was owned by T.J. Hicks & Co. In the background is Old Down Farm which has since become an extensive butter and cheese-making establishment.

165 A c. 1930 picture of The Old Down Inn situated at an important crossroads although the main Shepton Mallet to Bristol road originally took a less steep and more direct course from Gurney Slade, through what is now Emborough Pond, passing the east end of Emborough Church and across the fields to Ston Easton. This Inn was probably built when that road was redirected to its present line, possibly in the 1600's. However, the inn became an important centre for mail distribution with the London to Exeter Royal Mail coach stopping to collect mail and change horses from 1785 to 1841. Mail from overseas would also be brought here from Falmouth to be sorted. It was called the Red Lion in 1710, The Old Down Inn by 1774, and was a 'posting house' as early as 1760. It had its own postmark "Old-Down" from 1798 to 1841, and was gutted by a fire in 1885. Innkeepers during the last 100 years have been Ted Gait, Edward (Jim) Shorey, Edgar and Mary Hillman, Alex and Joy Dibble, Penny Dibble & Gordon Mashall (joint). There was once a double murder in the old kitchen of the inn.

165a   The annual scene outside the Old Down Inn on Druids Day (Whit Tuesday) before the traditional procession and other festivities (see 156/7 in Focus One) note also the large Lodge Banner, and the signpost on the Green pointing the original way to Shepton Mallet. Previously on the Green was a Horse-chestnut tree which was cut down in 1926.

166   A photo taken from the S & D railway embankment of the 19c viaduct at Marchants Hill which takes the A37 road over the deep valley at Emborough and on to Gurney Slade just over the rise. Up to the 1930's an overhead ropeway from Dalley's Quarry at Cockhill ran down the field on the left of the picture and was used to deposit stone into waiting trucks at the railway sidings which the quarry shared with Moorewood Colliery. On the other side of this road one can still find traces of Marchant's Hill Tollgate and lodge (1784) if one looks for the tell-tale clue of an area of nettles. This tollgate was at the junction of the pre-viaduct road and another road which came from Chilcompton to link with the first bend in Portway Lane (top centre) and this was the old road to Wells.

167 Part of the extensive premises of Emborough Quarry which was originally started as brickworks by T.J. Hicks & Co. when they closed their Old Down site (164). The tall figure is Robin Atthill, the Downside schoolmaster and historian who died 12/2/94. Victor Mogg was once in charge of the plant in this picture.

167a A c. 1880 scene at the quarry when most work was done by hand. The man in the centre is legless, quite common in early times, and is sitting on his own mode of transport. A different type of leglessness in those days was usually the result of local cider.

White Post and Norton Down

168 Staff at Norton Hall, home of the Beauchamp family at Norton Down, in the early 1900's. Only one name here—William Pointing on the left.

169 Herbert Carter, innkeeper of the White Post Inn during the 1910's and 1920's. He was succeeded by his son Alan, (MTC 200). Herbert's sister Alice married William Pearce, the Chilcompton village butcher.

170 Five smart young men gathered behind Mabel Rogers at White Post. Left to right—Bill Rogers, Dick and Bill Crook (brothers), Fred Rogers, and Percy Rogers (Mabel's twin).

171 Behind the White Post Inn in 1926. Sitting on the garden seat is Percy Rogers and little girl standing is Pearl Rogers. Behind are left to right—Grace Carter with her arm on Bill Crook's shoulder, Ewart Churchill, Nancy Carter, Alan Carter, George Rogers and Fred Rogers, Pearl's father.

171a Also behind the White Post Inn was a terrace of six houses all very basic with one communal outside tap, one washhouse, and "up the garden" lavatories. Mrs Emm Isom is pictured here with four of the houses behind.

172 The 1924 Christmas Day wedding of Percy Rogers and bride Elsie Gilson. Best man is Dick Crook and bride's father William Gilson. Front— Joyce (Ciss) Perkins, Mabel Rogers, May Goulden, and Christine Perkins. This was only the second wedding to take place at Norton Down Chapel. The first is featured in Focus One, 173.

173 The White Post Robbins football team, cupwinners in 1920. Standing—Sid Noad, Harry Sevior, Bert Champion. Middle—Seward Paradise, Ernie Atkins, Walt Perkins. Front—Alf Stedham, Bill Rogers, Percy Rogers (capt), Bert Dando, Percy Dando.

173a Three old ladies locked out of the lavatory— Bella Jones, Emm Isom and Sarah Cornick all from White Post around 1930.

173b A c. 1926 picture of what looks like a two-seater Tiger Moth resting in the field on 'Big Ground' the other side of the road to what is now Norton Rugby ground. The house in the background, The Firs, is still there. The pilot was apparently a beau of Mary Casswell who lived in the White Cottage nearby. Peter Beauchamp (later Sir) (Norton Hall) also owned a Tiger Moth for a time.

Stratton-on-the-Fosse

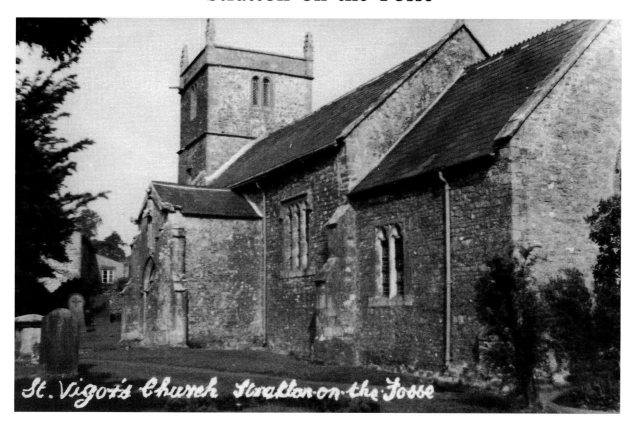

St. Vigor's Church Stratton-on-the-Fosse

174 and 175 There are only two churches in England dedicated to Saint Vigor—this one at Stratton and, below, the one at Fulbourn, Cambridgeshire. A history of St Vigor's church at Stratton was published in 1993.

176   An interesting part of old Stratton—The foreground has now made way for the Royal British Legion Club and car parks. Right foreground is a pair of houses which was formerly the vicarage. Behind these are St Vigor's Church and the Manor House. In the left background are six of the ten houses which formed a little estate called Church Row.

177   A group of pupils outside St Vigor's National School at Stratton c. 1904/5 with headmaster Mr Albert Woods. Percy Rogers stands third from the right in the back row, and his twin sister Mabel is sixth from the left in the 2nd row from the back (long fair hair). The school closed in Dec 1992 after 132 years.

177a A 1930's view of Downside Abbey and school with St Benedicts Church, school and nunnery behind the trees on the right. Sunnymead and Linkmead are further away.

177b A July 1993 photo of the same scene and readers will no doubt spend some time locating the many additions.

Interesting Letters

From Phyllis M. Edwards 1990

In 1911 I was born in Chilcompton vicarage and often visit the village now, having retired to Bath,. We left in 1915 as an economy measure. I was the first child to be born in the vicarage (I have been told) for 62 years. The bell ringers assembled in the church (stayed by my father's supplies of cider) but on hearing it was a girl they went home without ringing. On my brother's birth two and a half years later they rang a full Bob-minor (but perhaps that is a family hyperbole!).

I can tell you how the ghost was laid in the house the Matticks lent us in the street (Abingdon House) about 1916. Unknown to us when we arrived at the house, (mother, brother and I to escape the bombs of Bermondsey), it had been empty for some time because, according to previous tenants, it was haunted and footsteps in the night could be plainly heard. One night during a gale we heard the sound of breaking glass and the next morning, after a prolonged search, glass was found behind a large creeper outside. This creeper concealed a long forgotten window which had been plastered over on the inside and the 'ghost' noise was the creeper rubbing against the window.

It might be of interest to you to know that while at the vicarage my father instituted what was then a very modern system of illuminating the building. This was acetylene, set up in an outhouse, and piped to all rooms giving a brilliant light. The spent fuel was spread over the gravel drive which was much admired for being weed free!

From Nora Gilson 1984

My mother and father were both born in the village in 1869, and married at Christ Church Stockhill in 1896.

Mother was the daughter of the village police constable, Henry William Noble, living at the house next to the shop at the bottom of the village. After leaving school mother made her home with Mrs Ann Savage (mentioned in Kellys 1889) as a helper and shop assistant in the Hillside which became the home of Mr & Mrs Hoare. In those days the shop was well stocked with grocery, drapery and millinery. Mrs Savage a widow, was a splendid business woman and would get to Welton station for the journey to Bristol to buy her stock from the warehouses. A gentleman that came on holidays often to the village, presented the verse which he himself composed, to my mother and she would delight in reciting the words to her family right to the end of her 91 years.

My father, Jim Burge, was a gardener/handyman at Downside Lodge, a private nursing home for ladies of mental weakness, managed by Miss Constance Page who kept a staff of Cook, Parlour maid, Housemaid etc. I can remember the well kept grounds and flower beds the large vegetable garden and greenhouses full of beautiful plants. My father was quite an important character as he would drive Miss Page to visit her friends, to the shop & Post Office by donkey & governess cart. Also she was a good woman to the sick and aged, and he would deliver hot soup to some of the needy families in the village. I can remember how we would stand & admire the shining brass bridle on the donkey & brass decorations on the cart.

I shall always treasure the picture in my mind of the seven or eight colour washed cottages next to my home at Frys Well (Spring View) all of different design, with such tiny windows and such small living rooms, but quite a good sized back house (as it was called) which had a window that almost touched the road. As children we would kneel down to have a look in and run away.

There was no drainage, and their gardens quite small, every drop of water was poured on to the garden. The bucket toilets treated the same way.

Each cottage had a tiny wash house with the fire boiler built in the garden with the W.C. adjoining. The tenants were mostly miners from the New Rock Colliery also one or two widows who took in washing from the higher class families with water all to be carried from Frys Well in galvanised pails. The black smoke would pour from the drain pipe wash house chimney pots. They were fetching water all day long as did all the other cottages likewise. The washing of huge white sheets and other garments would dry and blow away on the clothes lines as white as snow and then one of the rewards was a walk to the Redan Inn with a jug for a half pint of frothy black stout.

I remember Mrs Elizabeth Coleman an excellent washer woman and Mrs Harry Lloyd both with such happy smiling red faces. The Public Houses were always full, a drunken man was quite a common sight. Harry Lloyd, I can well remember his struggle to walk home hanging on the wall for support.

My brother and two sisters now in late 70 years walked daily to Stockhill School, taking bread and butter sandwiches for dinner. Often my brother had eaten his on the journey & was left with no dinner unless his sisters shared a little with him. I was sent to school at Stratton - on-the-Fosse and walked through the fields until the age of fourteen years and we were taught by the Nuns who would take non-Catholics.

A great treat as a teenager was to see a silent film, kindly shown to public once weekly for 6d in the Downside College Gymnasium. The pianist was Mr George Maynard who gave the light touch of music for the sad moments and joyful tunes for the happy ones. People came from miles to see the films.

A sad event in my family was the receiving of a Police Court Summons to my brother for throwing stones, the boys would join together to see who could throw the stones over the top of Frys Well railway bridge and get them to drop on the other side of the road. My father was very much upset, but much relieved at the Court as there was no fine and the case dismissed.

Chilcompton was one of the first villages to have street lights. The oil lamps were erected in 1910 my fathers name was included in the list of applications for the job to attend to the care & keep going nightly the 9 lamps and he was given the post.

For many years he did this work through the winter months having to light them up in early evening and at 10 pm would go around to put them out.

Twice weekly they would be filled up with paraffin and once weekly the lamp glasses were cleaned on a Saturday's afternoon. Many a night a knock on the door from a villager would tell him a certain light was giving trouble and was smoking. He would leave his armchair and take his ladder to attend to it and so many times return home wet to the skin but they were times when the money was much appreciated.

The Church & Chapel had large congregations in my younger days with their choirs and other activities. Good times were spent at the Church House with a Girls Friendly Society. At one time I was a member and took part in a concert party visiting other villages with our singing, dialogues, monologues etc. A great treat was to ride on the train to Burnham-on-Sea on a Sunday School outing also to visit Radstock market on the train.

Then once a year a Chapel Bun Supper. Two large buns for each child full of fruit with wet sugar on top, held every year about February and a possible magic lantern show after.

Money was in short supply but they were happy days.

From Leslie Smailes who visited with Marion and Jane. 1991.

I write to thank you for the recent and most interesting 'Chilcompton conversations' and, because of the inopportune moment of our call, your kindness in delaying other arrangements to talk with us a little while. We do hope no one was inconvenienced.

And thankyou for the books!

We never thought, or expected that such would be obtainable – Two very excellent and interesting books – about Chilcompton –! A very pleasant surprise and enjoyed immensely. We scan the photographs in detail and find them quite fascinating – and sometimes, with a wee nostalgic twinge.

We hope, for you, that all Chilcompticans have bought them.

Earlier we had spoken with a very helpful lady living in the house adjacent to the Drang exit and it was she who suggested coming along to you: – "The very gentleman".

As children, in the 1920 days, we knew this row of houses as 'Veales'; our grocer and cobbler there, were, of course, Veales.

Our Grandmama was a Veale – Sarah Ann Smailes, neé Veale – but we knew her not, she going to her St Benedicts Plot, in 1915, when the writer, Leslie, was barely six months into his first century. Grandfather, a sailing ship man, had already been in occupation of his plot, in Fernando Po, for several years , while my father Gilbert

Ross and brother Ray, were still in their teens.

They lived together in a cottage at the bottom of the Drang - next to the one which, at present, is signed 'For Sale' and described as No. 2 Frys Well. For us it just used to be 'Down Shorts'.

My recollection has the hill from Wells Rd to the 'Well' as being 'Shorts Hill' – Tommy Short kept "The Redan".

We bought penny sweets there and had surreptitious sips of our elders cider. Other times we used the Drang, which was well surfaced , I think, and well used.

The 'Top Stile' was where we would collect with our bicycles, scooters and various wheeled constructions, to perform acrobatic feats and antics along the Wells Rd, from Bennell Batch to Shorts Hill. The daring thing was to ride down the Drang!

Looking at your photo No.88 of the young Veale children, there was excitement here at the 'recognising' of a very good 'resemblance' between Edna and our daughter Jane, when of a similar age. It could , of course be just coincidence-or be no more than 'imagination' – but Sarah Ann Smailes neé Veale was her Great-Grandma! We have no idea at all how she related to the other Veales of Frys Well and wondered if anyone, nowadays, could tell. Jane would be delighted to find herself with some 'removed' cousins down Chilcompton way.

We had lived at No 32 Wells Rd since it was built, circa 1915 and remained there until about 1926.

Our neighbours were the Jones's and the Raines, on either side and the Veales and the Golledges at either end of the row.

Mr Golledge was brother to builder Golledge and later, I think, re-opened my father's Cycle etc, business, in his own, end premises. A certainly much more suitable position.

The Veales, at the other end, had a young daughter with TB and we children were much concerned and would often make little presents for her.

Mr Raines was an elderly Railway man and a perfectionist gardener who really didn't deserve small boys as garden neighbours.

War-widow 'Jones' (to us), received good comfortings from my mother.

In picture 82, with your bedroom window just behind the Shell petrol sign, we can see that our No.32 front door is also sign - indicated and is the left most one just left of the RAC diamond.

Its unlikely that we were 'time share' neighbours as this would mean 'loading' you with far too many extra years!

I have various recollections of your house being built, but chiefly one of the uproar caused by my tumbling into the lime pool, which, in those days was a part of mortar making.

Previously there had been a large oak tree on the site and we sometimes played 'picnics' with the flat stump top as table.

Later, there were more houses beyond. One was for Miss Wall and her line of dog pens in the garden. Life was badger hunting. She would recount her sagas to us with total gusto. How times change.

Barton Drury's house, about opposite, now seems crowded out.

Your fine, back cover, aerial view, clearly shows the straight line part of the Stratton Path. I remember that it used to continue unswervingly to the Wells Rd Gate - which would place it very nearly alongside today's Petrol Pump position.

It was very pleasing to see the old Frys Well still in place, nicely restored and flowing as smoothly as ever.

Standing there beside it , I didn't even need to close my eyes to look back and evoke the scenes of long ago: The wives and maidens flocking down the hill with pails and pitchers, for bath water - and a little bit of gossip, afternoon time, before the 'coming-off-shift' of the new Rock Collierymen. Soon these miners, the sons and the husbands, would appear atop Shorts Hill: a hurrying noisy group, weary but still joking and laughing and showing the whites of their teeth and eye circles, in a fearsome contrast (to we youngsters), their completely coal-blackened persons.

They would come crowding down the slope with carbide lamps aswinging from the hand, and then separating off to the various cottages , and prepare for the rigorous, daily bathing ritual.

Some had a small stable-like wash-house at the rear, with a stone flagged floor and little else. Perhaps a door. For others it could be 'a tin bath affront the kitchen range'. Maybe there was a 'fancy' fold-away screen. Maybe there wasn't!

It was said that you could always tell a New Rock man because of his indelibly black rimmed eyes.

I think they mostly had the allotments that used to be there on the upper side of the Drang and which were very carefully tended and kept. I can still remember how we lads rated the soft fruit as the best in the village.

Fine weekends, during 'Shorts' midday openings, the 'chaps' , as they were called, would congregate along the, (then), low, Wells Rd wall of the pub, all in their Sunday Best, and with button-holes flowered, to yarn and brag and tussle. - and perhaps, to tease with returning churchgoers - some maybe, unlikely members of Tommy's 'congregation'

Eventually, they would depart, en masse, for an afternoon-long country ramble. (Always orderly). Most would usually cut a customary hazel stick to swish, or whittle a favoured pattern while going along.

Although my family had a regular habit of long Sunday walks, I cannot remember ever encountering the 'chaps' on our wanderings, or knowing just where they went. It was a matter of great mystery to we youngsters.

What my father did know however, on these walks, was the whereabouts of certain, highly magical, sweet bearing trees ! it was fabulous! Somehow he always managed to 'scent' another one, handy, whenever our footsteps lagged.

We never caught him out, but have since 'found' similar trees in Devon - and they give much joy. All round!

My Chilcompton memories are only way back, childhood ones, but your marvellous books are able to nudge out some long-stored and even quite forgotten, names and characters. I mention a few here as they come to mind:

Gerald Brady, who lived opposite. A good, studious, school friend.

Mabel Pointing, next row along from us, whom we all liked and were sometimes admonished to be as good as. Her brothers and sisters were older and inhabited another planet.

Albert Maggs, along Bennell Batch, with a covey of young, always laughing, daughters. Teresa and Winnie are two names.

Barton Drury, who sternly teased us.

The Stocks and the Churches lived down the drang. We climbed trees, feuded and explored.

Turk Burge, had a 'long distance' waist line.

Edna and Ada were 'down Veales'

Polly Emery, - 'down Turnpike' in her quaint little square house with exceeding tall chimney straight up from the middle. (Just visible in No 85).

Miss Sparrow. Was 'up the drive' - across Wells Rd from 'top 'o Shorts'. There with her Dachshund and tasty tea-scones.

Dr de Costabadie. A very kind gentleman and good friend of my mother's.

His son - over at Stratton. Possessed, for we children, a kind of aura, gained from his having lived in London.

Mrs (Leo) Jones and family, were 'Linkmeads'. Their sweet shop was always voted worth the trek.

The Carters, were nearby at The Gas House, with daughter Gladys - an absolutely charming and, so beautiful a young lady, of my own age group. (8/9) ?

Joyce Maggs, her same age cousin, at the Nettlebridge Inn... Even more beauteous and charming and delightful - absolutely the only girl in the world! I wonder where she is now.

The Perry's, also Linkmead, with a very nice, our age boy. Brother Stephen and self used to be dispatched on 'Playing Missions', but I think there was 'too much two to one'...!

My father, Gilbert 'Ross', was very much mechanically 'bent' (anything that went round and made a noise), and worked at Shearn's Norton Garage. He later went to New Rock, I think when the new Railway Siding was constructed.

It was possibly the General Strike that prompted him into the cycle shop venture at Wells Rd , but things were too restricted there.

The family moved on to Dorset, to a Farm Mechanisation Scheme, and thence to Salisbury, where father was very pleased with life at the Nestles Company, and we passed some very happy years in that beautiful city. Eventually we came to the Portsmouth area, and there my father enthusiastically and mechanically, passed his years - at the RNAS HMS "Daedalus", remaining there until his death in 1951.

By this time the family had 'grown up', (all with war service), and had started to disperse. To America, to Canada and to New Zealand - some even UK.

All had families except Fleet Air Arm Stephen, who didn't come back from the war.

All are now retired and all keep in regular touch.

All say they would love to make a trip to CHILCOMPTON.

Postscript

There were a few misprints in M.T.C. besides a number of faux pas most of which are corrected in the following passages. I have also included some additional information as I thought relevant. I recommend an early insertion of these misprints and corrections into my readers previous books to avoid misunderstandings.

Misprints Worth Mentioning

PAGE
32	Rockhill Lane.
39	Doug Flower was the last innkeeper at Naish's Cross Inn.
59	The Carver family was at Prospect Place.
70	Georgina Bodman.
82	Mr Jacob.
136	George Osmond.
167	1921 Jan. Miss Esther Moore.

Corrections to M.T.C.

PAGE
xv	Margery Vinnell.
2	The 'River Somer' imposed upon it in the latter half of the 19th century.
3	Wellow Brook.
8	Although spelt Epsley in old records he was actually Thomas Hippisley. James Tooker was High Sheriff in 1766.
10	Tom Paine was not a notorious local highwayman; he was a Norfolk born author who became unpopular because of his apparent lack of patriotism. He died in New York in 1809 aged 72.
17	Mill Spring and Marsh Spring were more likely situated by the mill near the Parish Church. The pre-1984 Mill Cottage was similar in size to today's but was flanked by larger ancillary buildings.
32, 94	Oliver Major Tapp was a name and not a military rank.
50	(bottom of page) The shop was under Stan's genial leadership for 40 years until1971. It was then a newsagents shop with proprietor Ken Wellington until it finally closed in 1973.
52, 74	Arthur and Reuben Dunford's shop was built in 1938.

60	The cottage was just below, north, of the R.C. Church.
68	Compton Beeches. It was 1816 before the 'front door' road diversion (The Street) was officially applied for although it was already drawn on the 1784 map.
91	Mr White had not lived in Shell House Farm.
103	Mr Fred James died in 1924 before he could move into 'Westholme' so his son Charles lived there instead from 1924-52.
145	Mr Charles Mattick was Warden for 43 years.
156	In 1903 a Village Hall was given by Downside Abbey Trustees and erected on a plot of land in lower Chilcompton on what is now the entrance to Upper Pitching estate. The hall was little used because the area was prominently Anglican so on 1st May 1911 it was dismantled, moved and rebuilt on what is now St Aldhelm's Church forecourt at a cost of £78-11-0. The excellent 'disappearing' billiard table had been purchased from Oakhill School.
166	(1915) Norton Hill School, which had been opened on the 6th May 1912 was from January 1915 to September 1916 shared with wounded soldiers who were cared for on the top floor.
203	Mrs Mabel Plumley's husband drove a locomotive hauling coal trucks between Norton Hill Colliery and the Railway. Mabel is now 105 in 1994.
218	Norton Green Farmhouse and cottage.
226	Brook House Farm.
245	A restless mind makes a ruffled pillow. (How true!).

ADDITIONAL INFORMATION (M.T.C.)

Regarding Chil or Childe—Childars were the sons of War Lords who inhabited the coombes between the hills about 400 AD.

8	A certain Mr Whiteacre was a pipe maker in Chilcompton from 1670 to 1674
9	Another moonbow was recorded by John Golledge on 15th August 1946 and on 5th September 1987 another was seen by several Chilcomptonians including myself.
18	The Mill near Somer House was used by James Padfield as a base for making edge tools from 1840 to 1899. He was the founder of the three generations of Padfields who worked their forges for nearly 100 years. James lived in a house in the rear terrace of Britania Yard and was succeeded in his work by his son William who moved to Brook House in 1899 where he worked two forges and exported some of his tools as far afield as Russia. In 1902 he moved again to his own newly-built

premises in Baker's Lane, now called Bevois House. Helped by two of his 10 children, William and Curtis, he continued edge toolmaking almost until he died in 1937. His son Curtis (A.C.Padfield) continued the name in a wider range of commodities almost until he died in 1979. (See also pages 45 and 89.)

23   The name 'Pines Express' came from the wooded area the train passed through on leaving Bournemouth.

27   The A37 toll-gate was called Marchants Hill Gate in 1784.

33   One or two old timers have since insisted that when they were boys and went down pitching they were referring to a game of pitching coins.

36   Another Britania Innkeeper about 1920 was Bernard Gladstone (Gladdie) Burge.

38   The pre-1855 name for the Redan Inn was the 'The Sheppards Rest'.

40   The Sword and Castle was closed in 1986, sold to the Wadworth Brewery, re-named the Somerset Wagon and re-opened on Monday 30th November 1987. The new innkeeper Terry Sage (late village postmaster) and I planted an oak sapling on that day at the rear as a commemoration.

48   The concrete works were started in 1926.

54   W.W. Pearce took over the butchers shop from his uncle Arthur John Gait before moving into his new premises (picture).

58   My old friends the Dally family also lived at Frys Well.

59   There was also a detached house situated behind the rear terrace of Britannia Yard; one of its last occupants was John Raynes in the early 1800's.

60   There was also a cottage in the farmyard just south of the Wintertop Farm where the Perry's and 'Punch' Cottle had lived.

63   The splendid stone barn gutted by fire has now been restored.

66   The Stockers are reputed to have come from Cork.

67   Plans and sketches of the Manor House are on pages 64, 65 & 254.

77   Underneath a plastered wall at Gainsborough House there is reputed to be a drawing of some importance.

90   For many years a room at Waterloo Farm was used for vestry and other church meetings.

93   Another Downside Abbey Home Farm manager was Frank Drew.

94   Gilbert Leach was at Old Rock Farm from Christmas 1905 to 22nd February 1916. His wife Beatrice was born 24th December 1881 at Naishes Cross Inn, where her father William Tapp was landlord. Her brother was Oliver Tapp. A Mr Flagg was another tenant after Gilbert.

104   (Top of page.) A certain Hopton Stocker also enlisted.

125   Sweetleaze Colliery, 4th line. On 26th August 1858 a resolution was made to open out the Great Course Seam by means of an incline plane at Sweetleaze, but it was 1861 before it was re-opened.

132   The Church was publicly re-opened on Wednesday 18th September 1839 with an 11am Service and sermon by Revd. Edward Tottenham, M.A., and a 2.30pm Service by Revd John W.Watts, M.A. Unfortunately the materials used in the restoration were such that the Nave and Chancel were condemned in the 1890s as being unsafe with a colossal damp problem, so the work was due to be done again. However the builders of that era,1897-8, managed to save the Nave except for re-roofing , but the Chancel had to be rebuilt. See Restoration Fund particulars 133 .

133   Churchwardens are usually elected every year.

135   An entry in the Churchwardens Accounts from April 1844-45 states 'The Revd G. Newnham gave £3-10-0 to buy a new font from Coombe Down'.

136   The Choir seats were erected in March 1903.

141   The two Glebe Fields on the east side of lower Stockhill have since been sold to Douglas Flower.

142   The Revd Henry Whittington died on 13th November 1899 after 44 years as vicar. Owing to his age, a curate Revd Revel Green was appointed to assist him from 1895-1900. The Revd H.P. Leakey successor to Revd H. Whittington, died on 16th April 1902 at Bath and was buried at Ston Easton. The Revd A .A. Brockington was instituted on 11th may 1903 and inducted on 27th July 1903. Revd W. Page was inducted on the 11th December 1905 and died on 21st October 1909.

162   Two Conscientious Chapel caretakers during the 1940s and 50s were Stan and Evelyn Perkins.

208   Gilbert Prior and Fred Penny also worked for the Hignells at Killings Knap. Albert (Jack) and Gladys Mears lived at Killings Knap - the house facing Stratton - from Feb 1938-1949. Gladys taught at St Vigors School from 1945-73.

219   Eli Grigg was another knife and scissor sharpener.

225   Farrington Gurney market closed in 1971.

228   Ruth Dunford and Christine Mattick were also Girl Guide leaders. The old mill at Slade Bottom was last used by Oliver Gait as a cornmill. Other large families include Davis 11, Perkins 11, Schuster 9, and two more Padfields 9 and 8.

235   On the night of 16th October 1940 a German Dornier bomber crashed on the summit of Maesbury Ring killing the four man crew.

246   Fry's Well provided many generations with drinking water. In 1973 the large front riser stone was broken by sewerage contractors and was replaced by a 7cwt piece of Balmoral Red Granite. Work was carried out by R.J. Ham of Wells.

Corrections to Focus One

Readers of this book may also have a copy of CHILCOMPTON IN FOCUS ONE (1989) in which a few mistakes also occurred and these are outlined in the following script:

In my Preface I said that I had started the book with views of the old village, but these views became relegated to pages 34 and 35.

24   The tractor was seen as early as 1924.

32   The Peppard family were pictured at their home at Middle Street, East Harptree some of the daughters were wrongly named. Corrected they are: left to right - Rosena (in arms), Florence, Kate, Beatrice, Eva and Mary (Jun).

33   This picture of the Webber family became inverted and therefore reads from right to left.

45   Not Bob and Sally but Pam and Pete Gilson.

53   The driver is Will Dart.

61   The names of the Christ Church Choir were inadvertently omitted and are as follows: Back Curtis Padfield, Bert Gibbings, Bill Ridout, Bill Nash, Bill Gibbings, Harold Witcombe.
Middle Charlie Gilson, Arthur Gilson, Les Dowling, Jess Upward, Hilary Upward, Henry (Sonny) Flagg, Ivan Flagg.
Front Ruth Clarke, Grace Witcombe, Miss E.J. Jones, Rev'd Thomas Wilberforce Upward, Edith Dyke, Sarah Llewellyn, Gwen Coles, Gwen Gibbings.
Squatting Joe Dring, Sidney Spratt, Jim Olney.

67   The missing name was Marjorie Baker.

76   The missing name was Valerie Kelly

110   Second Column, first para. – A line from Nobby Uphill's interesting letter has been left out and it should read:

'Years ago there was a brickyard at the back of the Court Hotel also the turnpike used to be at the bottom of Lynch Hill then later another was built at the Coal Lane entrance.'